ESSENTIALLY

D0104827

DESIGN: Eliana Stein

ACKNOWLEDGMENTS

Thanks first and foremost to the folks who manage the 826 stores: Justin Allan, Justin Carder,
Christina Galante, Daniel Johnson, Joshua Martin, Patrick Shaffner, and Amy Sumerton.
Thanks to 826 staff, volunteers, interns, and designers. This catalog represents just a small
portion of the work that they do. And for modeling the T-shirts and other odds and ends, thanks
to Tracey Cooper, Darren Franich, Eli Horowitz, Elizabeth Kohout, Greg Larson, Juliet Litman,
Kyle O'Loughlin, Lindsay Quella, Megan Rickel, Cherylle Taylor, and Chris Ying.

826 NATIONAL STAFF: Nínive Calegari, Lauren Hall, Ryan Lewis, and Yvonne Wang.

ISBN: 978-1-934750-09-4

ESSENTIALLY
ODD

a catalog of products created for
and sold at the 826 stores

TO ORDER

Most—nearly all!—of the products in this catalog are available online. To order, visit the Web site of the 826 store that carries your product or visit **www.826national.org/stores** for links to every store.

826 Boston
THE GREATER BOSTON BIGFOOT RESEARCH INSTITUTE
www.826boston.org

826 Chicago
THE BORING STORE
www.notasecretagentstore.com ◆ 773.772.8108

826LA
THE ECHO PARK TIME TRAVEL MART
www.826la.org/store ◆ 213.413.3388

826michigan
THE LIBERTY STREET ROBOT SUPPLY & REPAIR
www.826michigan.org/store

826NYC
THE BROOKLYN SUPERHERO SUPPLY CO.
www.superherosupplies.com

826 Seattle
THE GREENWOOD SPACE TRAVEL SUPPLY CO.
www.greenwoodspacetravelsupply.com

826 Valencia
THE PIRATE SUPPLY STORE
www.826valencia.org/store ◆ 415.642.5905 ext.201

INTRODUCTION

826 NATIONAL IS A NETWORK OF YOUTH TUTORING AND WRITING CENTERS with locations in seven cities—San Francisco, Los Angeles, Brooklyn, Boston, Chicago, Ann Arbor and Seattle. At the core of the organization is a dedication to helping students 6–18 with their English and writing skills. The idea when the organization started, back in 2002, was a simple one—provide one-on-one tutoring for students falling behind— but along the way there were some strange detours. Those detours led us to create odd storefronts that sold odder products—peg legs, robot emotions, caveman food, and space-travel underwear, among hundreds of other semi-useful things. How did this happen? And is this a good idea?

Back in the fall of 2001, Dave Eggers and some friends and were looking to rent a space on Valencia Street in San Francisco's Mission District. They planned to open an after-school tutoring center for the kids who lived in the neighborhood; it was a simple and only semi-formed notion. The plan was that the front of the building would be used for tutoring and workshops, and the back would house the offices of McSweeney's, their small publishing house.

When they looked into the building they wanted to use at 826 Valencia Street, the landlord was open to the idea of a tutoring center, but he told Dave that the address was zoned for retail. They had no choice, the landlord said: at the front of the building, they had to sell something.

The space had been a weight room in the mid 90s, and after that had housed a comics store/importer-exporter of Japanese comics. It had a very corporate look—drop ceilings of acoustic tile, and rubber floors (from the weight room days). When Eggers and Co. took down the acoustic tile, they found beautiful wooden beams, old and white-washed. When they pulled up the rubber flooring, they found almost perfect wood floors. Very soon, the building had taken on the look of the hull of an old ship.

Someone said, "You know what you should sell? Pirate supplies." It made everyone laugh, but it made no sense at all. Then again, selling anything at the front of a tutoring center didn't seem to make any sense, either. So they went with the idea, and built the rest of the space to look as pirate-supply-shop-y as possible.

Early on, the 826 founders decided that the shop should serve *working* pirates, as opposed to being a kitschy shop *about* pirates. The difference was simple. Instead of products with pictures of pirates on them, they would sell things that an actual pirate might buy—from maps to sextants to lard. The products had to be period-specific, too. Nothing plastic, nothing cheap-looking. So Yosh Han, the first pirate-store manager, developed relationships with a wide range of wholesalers, who provided the store with goods of wood, copper, rope, glass and steel. At the same time, the volunteers at 826 Valencia began making their own products. Using toilet plungers and handkerchiefs, they made beautiful custom-fitted peg legs. They packaged beard extensions, created special-occasion eye patches, and created a line of planks for all weights and eventualities.

Soon the store had its own distinct aesthetic and even a certain mythology. The work was fun. Creating the store was fun for the volunteers, and the fun rubbed off on the students who came to 826 Valencia for tutoring help. Soon a good majority of the volunteers and students had come through the

PLAN OF A TYPICAL 826

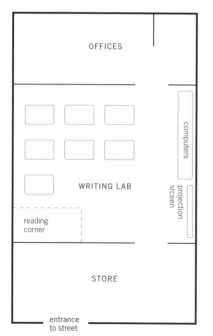

storefront. They would walk in off the street, curious to see the bizarre shop, and would learn about the programs and opportunities happening just behind the store.

So when groups started sister 826 centers in other cities, they used the same model—a storefront facing the street and welcoming the community at large, and in the back, plenty of room for desks, chairs, field trips, workshops, and one-on-one learning. And the storefronts were as varied as the cities themselves. In New York they opened the Brooklyn Superhero Supply Co., LA's storefront is the Echo Park Time Travel Mart, Chicago's Boring Store sells spy gear, Seattle boasts the Greenwood Space Travel Supply Co., Michigan is fronted by The Liberty Street Robot Supply and Repair Store, and Boston has the The Greater Boston Bigfoot Research Institute.

Each 826 center worked with local artists and designers to craft a distinct fantasy retail environment. Local creative types would leap in to conjure a wonderful world that would delight customers and intrigue kids, and the products they created, when sold, would help pay the rent on the buildings. And that's the real bottom-line benefit of the storefronts: they really do help provide a predictable revenue source. Just as monks often sell honey or vegetables to support their monastic life, so can the 826 centers ensure their longevity by selling secret identity kits and viking-scented odorant. The story of the 826 National storefronts is a lesson in how nonprofits have to stay flexible and creative to survive, and to achieve some kind of financial independence.

This catalog presents a sampling of the best products available at the various stores. It's a showcase of insane creativity on the part of local designers, artists and craftspeople making strange things for a good cause. All the products herein are for sale, and all sales are not only final but should, upon arrival, be considered the buyer's favorite thing they own. The proceeds from every purchase will benefit the students in one of seven cities across the country, so thank you so much for supporting 826 National.

826 VALENCIA

826 VALENCIA
THE PIRATE SUPPLY STORE

It should be noted that the pirate store at 826 Valencia is the only independent buccaneer purveyor in the San Francisco Bay Area. Our main competitor is Captain Rick's Booty Cove, a huge corporate pusher of inferior products. Please do not shop at Captain Rick's! Even his lard is bad, and it's hard to make bad lard.

Exterior Designer: Dave Eggers • *Mural Designer:* Chris Ware
Interior Designer: Dave Eggers • *Logo Designer:* Office, visitoffice.com
Store Manager: Justin Carder
826 VALENCIA STREET, SAN FRANCISCO, CALIFORNIA
WWW.826VALENCIA.ORG

PINK EYE

DYSENTERY

GANGRENE

PINK EYE

Bone Soup

JUST ADD WATER

DECENT
PEG
LEG
OIL

DECENT
PEG
LEG
OIL

DECENT
PEG
LEG
OIL

GLA

DR

826 VALENCIA: PROGRAM OVERVIEW

OPENED: April 2002

SERVES: San Francisco Unified School District

NEIGHBORHOOD: The Mission District

NUMBER OF VOLUNTEERS: 1,410

MOST RECENT PUBLICATION: *Show of Hands: Young Authors Reflect on the Golden Rule*—written by 54 juniors and seniors at Mission High School

SATELLITES: Writers' Rooms at Everett Middle School and James Lick Middle School

FIELD TRIPS HOSTED: 118 in 2007–08

IN-SCHOOLS SESSIONS: 526 in 21 schools in 2007–08

WORKSHOPS OFFERED: 36 in 2007–08

TOTAL NUMBER OF STUDENTS SERVED: 6,065

TUTORING SPACE: 2,100 square feet

STAFF: Justin Carder, Emilie Coulson, Marisa Gedney, Eugenie Howard-Johnston, Jory John, Leigh Lehman, María Inés Montes, and Cherylle Taylor

NOTES: *We collaborated with the team at 826 Valencia to develop a new identity and nearly 50 exclusive products. We tried to create an authentic, visually cohesive story, inspired by the idea of a 18th century pirate walking into a 21st century store to pick up a few things. All the labels and signs were printed on thick uncoated stock using silver and gold ink. —Office*

WRITER: Office, Dave Eggers
DESIGNER: Office, visitoffice.com

ITEM NUMBER: 826SF 100
ITEM NAME: Blackwater Fever
SPECIFICATIONS: 5.5" x 2" x 2"
WRITER: Office, Dave Eggers
DESIGNER: Office, visitoffice.com
PRICE: $8.00

NOTES: *This is one of the great products that Office came up with. After they had designed the packaging, we just went in and toned down some of the language. It's over-tempting to use the "arrgh" and "blimey" sort of pirate-speak, and our goal became to make all the copy sound plain and almost unintentionally funny. These pills are guaranteed (probably) to do something about your Blackwater Fever, the deadliest of pirate ailments.*

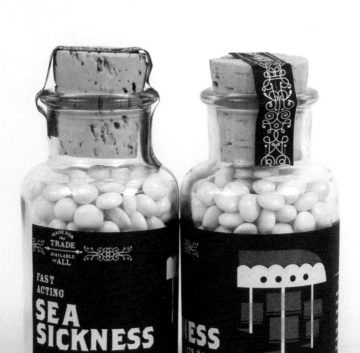

ITEM NUMBER: 826SF 101
ITEM NAME: Sea Sickness Tablets
SPECIFICATIONS: 4.25" x 2" x 2"
WRITER/DESIGNER: Office,
visitoffice.com
PRICE: $8.00

NOTES: *Fast-acting sea sickness tablets quickly quell queasiness, nausea, hardtack-belly and hammock spins to help keep you on an even keel.*

ITEM NUMBER: 826SF 102
ITEM NAME: Scurvy Begone
SPECIFICATIONS: 5.5" x 2.25" x 2.25"
WRITER/DESIGNER: Office,
visitoffice.com
PRICE: $9.00

NOTES: *Each capsule contains the power of one entire lime or lemon, to rid you of scurvy. Fairly probable side effects: hirsutism; supernumerary organs; chimerism; sudden onset of fake English accent; boils.*

a
b   c

ITEM NUMBER: a. 826SF 103, b. 826SF 104, c. 826SF 105

ITEM NAME: a. Pink Eye Leeches, b. Dysentery Leeches, c. Gangrene Leeches

SPECIFICATIONS: 4" x 2.5" x 2.5"

WRITER/DESIGNER: Office, visitoffice.com

PRICE: $13.00 each

NOTES: *These are jars full of fake leeches. We actually use the same fake leeches, I think, as 826LA.*

- *Guaranteed to make a serious attempt at reducing some of the disadvantages of having dysentery.*
- *Guaranteed to try very hard to relieve you of the more noticeable aspects of gangrene.*
- *Guaranteed to make you feel like you've tried to do something about your pink eye.*

On the bottle:

BUCANEROS DE VALENCIA

⊹ DECENT ⊹

PEG
LEG
OIL

BENEFITS OF A WELL
...D PEG LEG

...your leg an
...ce that says
...alk quickly
...ecessary"

...prevent dry rot

...against damage
...n and salt

...water-resistance
...lick conditions

ITEM NUMBER: 826SF 106
ITEM NAME: Decent Peg Leg Oil
SPECIFICATIONS: 5" x 2.5" x 2.5"
WRITER/DESIGNER: Office,
visitoffice.com
PRICE: $7.00

NOTES: *I started liking the word "decent" in products. I made a can of rocks—just a can of rocks—and called it "DECENT ROCKS" and kind of liked how candid it was. So then we added the word "decent" to Office's great Peg Leg Oil product. Designed to bring even the most wizened wood back to its original sheen, it works on pine, oak, Danish teak, mahogany and driftwood. —Dave Eggers*

ITEM NUMBER: 826SF 107
ITEM NAME: Eau de Mer
SPECIFICATIONS: 5.5" x 4.5" x 2.5"
WRITER/DESIGNER: Office,
visitoffice.com
PRICE: $30.00

NOTES: *Eau de Mer cologne no. 12 was blended especially pour homme (pirates specifically), with water and sediment from our own San Francisco Bay. Each limited edition bottle includes the following inscription:* Love is not a rogue wave to be breached. Love is a turtle to be lured into a rowboat, clubbed, quartered and devoured. The scent of mystery has seldom smelled so tangy.

15

ITEM NUMBER: 826SF 108

ITEM NAME: Bone Soup

SPECIFICATIONS: 7.5" x 4" x 4"

WRITER/DESIGNER: Office, visitoffice.com

PRICE: $18.00

NOTES: *Developed in the Dead Sea and passed along for generations, finally available without a license. Hormone-free and an excellent source of calcium.*

ITEM NUMBER: 826SF 109
ITEM NAME: Message in a Bottle
SPECIFICATIONS: 5.75" x 2.5" x 2.5"
WRITER: Office, Dave Eggers
DESIGNER: Office, visitoffice.com
PRICE: $15.00

NOTES: *Good for staying in touch with friends and wives, requesting rescue and expressing your thoughts and feelings.*

ITEM NUMBER: 826SF 110
ITEM NAME: Gold Tooth
SPECIFICATIONS: 4" x 2.5"
WRITER: Office
DESIGNER: Office, visitoffice.com
PRICE: $5.00

NOTES: *Plundered from the mouths of his defeated enemies, these gold (colored) teeth are from the private collection of the dread John Quelch.*

ITEM NUMBER: 826SF 111
ITEM NAME: Temporary Tattoos
SPECIFICATIONS: 5" x 3.25"
WRITER: Office
DESIGNER: Office, visitoffice.com
PRICE: $5.00 for each tattoo

NOTES: *For the commitment-averse buccaneer, these tattoos depict illustrations never seen before on the skin or elsewhere. All original designs by Office.*

CAPTAIN BLACKBEARD'S
BEARD EXTENSIONS.

PATCHY SPOTS GOT YA DOWN?
FEAR NOT,
CAPT. BLACKBEARD GROWS 'EM WHERE YOU CAN'T.

So silky the ladies will swoon.
So coarse your crew will covet.

ITEM NUMBER: 826SF 112
ITEM NAME: Captain Blackbeard's Beard Extensions
SPECIFICATIONS: varies, approx. 6" x 4"
WRITER/DESIGNER: Office, visitoffice.com
PRICE: $8.00

NOTES: *The length of a seaman's beard is in many ways the measure of the man. So for those who don't grow facial hair well, fast, or at all, these extensions are life-savers. Available in many sizes and textures and levels of filthiness.*

a   b

ITEM NUMBER: a. 826SF 113, b. 826SF 114
ITEM NAME: a. Kicking Sand,
b. Treasure Burial Sand
SPECIFICATIONS: 6" x 2.5" x 2.5"
WRITER/DESIGNERS: Justin Carder,
Walter Green
PRICE: a. $6.00, b. $9.00

NOTES: *We had a line of sands that we claimed was from all over the world but was actually the same sand with different labels. It upset a lot of real-life sand collectors. After months passed without a sale, we held a competition to repackage the sand. And thus was born Kicking Sand (for kicking into eyes), Beard Sand (for people who hate the beach but need to look like they love it), Sand of Time, and finally, Emergency Treasure Burial Sand.*
—Walter Green

ITEM NUMBER: 826SF 115
ITEM NAME: Sea Salt of the Seven Seas
SPECIFICATIONS: 6.5" x 6.5" x 2"
WRITER/DESIGNER: Dave Eggers
PRICE: $28.00

NOTES: *This is real salt. It's not necessarily from seven different seas, but in any case, this is a pretty popular item. The catch with many of the products in our stores is their utility: most of them aren't actually so useful. But this one offers actual cooking salt, and the containers can be used for any kind of spice or animal innards. —D.E.*

a

b   c

ITEM NUMBER: a.826SF 116,
b. 826SF 117, c. 826SF 118
ITEM NAME: a. Pine Needle Tea,
b. Cannon Fuses,
c. Mermaid Bait or Repellent
SPECIFICATIONS: 2" x 2.5" x .5"
WRITER/DESIGNER: Justin Carder
PRICE: $4.00 each

NOTES: *The tins came about because I wanted to design a line of products that could be kept in a pocket or stuffed into a boot and easily carried around. The first I put together was Cannon Fuses. In the 18th century, most fuses were made out of pieces of paper or cloth twisted up and filled with gun powder. Blackbeard got his name by tying them into his beard so he would be ready for battle at all times. Next we did Pine Needle Tea (one of the oldest cures for scurvy) and lastly Mermaid Bait or Repellent. —Justin Carder*

ITEM NUMBER: 826SF 119
ITEM NAME: Parrot Plank
SPECIFICATIONS: 12" x 1.25" x .25"
WRITER/DESIGNER: Dave Eggers
PRICE: $5.99

ITEM NUMBER: 826SF 120
ITEM NAME: Kitten Plank
SPECIFICATIONS: 24" x 3.5" x .75"
WRITER/DESIGNER: Dave Eggers
PRICE: $9.99

ITEM NUMBER: 826SF.121
ITEM NAME: Hamster Plank
SPECIFICATIONS: 24" x 2.5" x .75"
WRITER/DESIGNER: Dave Eggers
PRICE: $9.99

ITEM NUMBER: 826SF 122
ITEM NAME: Monkey Plank
SPECIFICATIONS: 23" x 8.5" x .75"
WRITER/DESIGNER: Dave Eggers
PRICE: $12.99

NOTES: *I went on a new product kick in the summer of '08. We hadn't really had any new products in the store for many years, so when Office started doing theirs, I got inspired and made some new ones, too. This was the first line I made, in about an hour one day. I bought a bunch of wood at the hardware store and thought of the appropriate animals for each plank. The labels were admittedly a bit underdone, but I wanted to get them done quickly, using one of the fonts Office had chosen. People get upset about the Kitten Plank. People don't have a problem with the Hamster Plank or Parrot Plank, but the Kitten Plank makes some people mad. —D.E.*

BAD NAMES FOR YOUR SHIP

- THE CONTENTED FELLA
- THE THICK-WAISTED LADY
- S.S. INNOCUOUS
- THE PAUNCHY
- OUR SLOW BUT STEADY BOAT
- JACQUI

ITEM NUMBER: 826SF 123
ITEM NAME: Complete Buccaneer Signage Kit
SPECIFICATIONS: 10" x 10" x 4"
WRITER/DESIGNER: Dave Eggers
PRICE: $30.00

NOTES: *The first thing we sold at the pirate store were these signs. Back in 2002, I wrote some, Eli Horowitz wrote some, my brother Toph wrote some. No new ones had been written in many years, so I did some new ones, and we added some actual archival pirate rules and regulations (each ship had its own code of conduct). The package also comes with a booklet,* Things You Should Know About Captain Rick, *which is a book of libelous statements about the guy who runs our chain store competition,* Captain Rick's Booty Cove. —D.E.

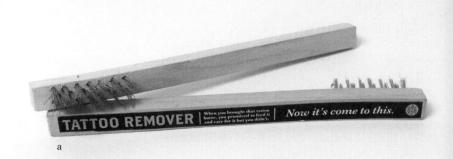

a

b

ITEM NUMBER: a. 826SF 124,
b. 826SF 125
ITEM NAME: a. Tattoo Remover,
b. Turtle Stunner
SPECIFICATIONS: a. 8" x .5" x .5",
b. 7.5" x 2.5" x 1.25"
WRITER/DESIGNER: a. Justin Carder,
b. Dave Eggers
PRICE: a. $7.00, b. $8.99

NOTES: *The stunner happened the same weekend as the planks. I went to Cost-Plus one Saturday and bought a bunch of tools and objects, and then went home to figure out how to re-purpose each one. I loved the look of this little meat tenderizer, and had been reading about various shipwreck victims, who always seemed to survive by eating turtles who were dumb enough to swim up to the rafts or rowboats lost at sea. —D.E.*

ITEM NUMBER: 826SF 126
ITEM NAME: Brain Bucket
SPECIFICATIONS: 5.5" x 4.5" x 6"
WRITER/DESIGNER: Dave Eggers
PRICE: $16.99

NOTES: *Sometimes one's brain falls out, and one needs a place to put it, or catch it. This is a bucket for brains. It comes in another size, too—Brain Bucket Jr.—but our supplier went bankrupt and we now have no source of tiny buckets.*

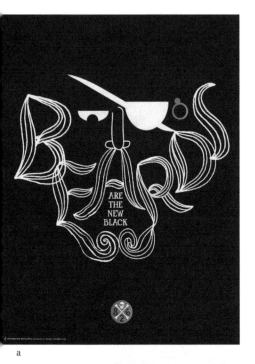

a

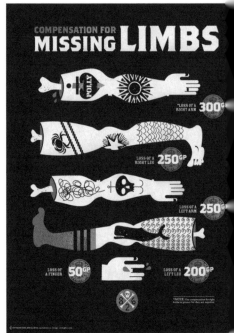

b

c

d

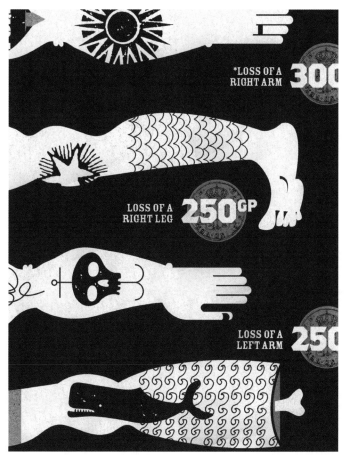

*LOSS OF A
RIGHT ARM 300

LOSS OF A
RIGHT LEG 250GP

LOSS OF A
LEFT ARM 250

b - detail

ITEM NUMBER: a. 826SF 128, b. 826SF
129, c. 826SF 130, d. 826SF 131
ITEM NAME: a. Beard Poster,
b. Limbs Poster, c. Plunder Poster,
d. Cannons Poster
SPECIFICATIONS: 26" x 20"
Gold and white ink on black paper
WRITER: Office
DESIGNER: Office, visitoffice.com
PRICE: $20.00 each

NOTES: *We illustrated a limited edition series of posters.
Our favorite is based on an actual insurance policy,
outlining the compensation for limbs lost at sea (e.g., 300
gold pieces for a right arm; 250 for a left.)*

Each of these designs is also available on a T-shirt.

ITEM NUMBER: 826SF 002
ITEM NAME: Cannons T-shirt
SPECIFICATIONS: 100% cotton
WRITER: Office
DESIGNER: Office, visitoffice.com
PRICE: $20.00

NOTES: *All poster designs from the previous page are available as T-shirts.*

ITEM NUMBER: 826SF 001
ITEM NAME: 826 T-shirt
SPECIFICATIONS: 100% cotton
DESIGNER: Office, visitoffice.com
PRICE: $20.00

826NYC
THE BROOKLYN SUPERHERO SUPPLY CO.

The Brooklyn Superhero Supply Company is the one-stop shopping destination for any being in need of powerful tools of the crime-fighting trade. Our goal is to provide customers with every imaginable resource, from basic capes and masks to high-tech particle rifles and potent canisters of Justice. In addition to these essential items, we also offer free in-store services, such as a full-featured Cape Tester and supremely effective De-Villainizer Unit.

Exterior: Work AC · *Storefront:* Sam Potts · *Interior Designers:* Sam Potts and Scott Seeley
Logo Designer: Sam Potts, sampottsinc.com
Store Manager: Joshua Martin
372 Fifth Avenue, Brooklyn, New York
www.826NYC.org

OUTFITTING

ORDER DIRE[CT]
[F]ROM THE
[WA]REHOUS[E]

[R]OT ARMIES
[A]ND NEW IN STOCK

[CYB]ORG
[ASSE]MBLY
[KI]T

[...]E AVAILABLE

[...]-BASED
[DRI]LLS

[...]D TODAY

[...]APE
[SUI]TS

[HA]LVED

[...]RY
[...]N CAMP
[...]EMENT

O[...]ING M[...] SOLD SEPARATELY

[...]SED
[...]ROES

[...]EATH RAYS
[...]OISY LASERS
[...]ERATURES

SECRET
IDENTITY
KITS

[VI]TAL

826NYC: PROGRAM OVERVIEW

OPENED: June 2004

SERVES: New York City public schools

NEIGHBORHOODS: Park Slope and Williamsburg

NUMBER OF VOLUNTEERS: 830

MOST RECENT PUBLICATION: *Behind the Uniforms*—an anthology of illustrated fiction, cartoons, and true stories written and edited by students of the Academy of College Preparation and Career Exploration

SATELLITE: Tutoring center at the Williamsburg branch of the Brooklyn Public Library

FIELD TRIPS HOSTED: 67 in 2006–07

IN-SCHOOLS SESSIONS: 37 in 2006–07

WORKSHOPS OFFERED: 41 in 2006–07

TOTAL NUMBER OF STUDENTS SERVED: 2,561

TUTORING SPACE: 1,720 square feet

STAFF: Kate Ackerman, Joan Kim, Joshua Martin, Anthony Mascorro, Sarah Pollock, Chris Roberti, Scott Seeley, and Ted Thompson

a

b

ITEM NUMBER: a. 826NYC 100, b. 826NYC 101, c. 826NYC 102, d. 826NYC 104
ITEM NAME: a. Gravity, b. Antimatter, c. Muscle, d. Speed of Light
SPECIFICATIONS: a. 7.5" x 6.5" x 6.5", b. 4" x 3.5" x 3.5", c. 4.75" x 4.25" x 4.25", d. 7.5" x 2.5" x 2.5"
WRITERS: 826NYC team
DESIGNER: Sam Potts
PRICE: a. $14, b. $10.99, c. $12.99, d. $14

c

d

NOTES: *The general concept for the Brooklyn Superhero Supply Company store, from the beginning, was that it was a kind of Lowe's or Wal-Mart for Superheroes. It would be the place where heroes could come get all the necessities imaginable that one might need for crime-fighting at unbeatable prices. So, we knew that our flagship line had to have that generic feel to it—as though there were a bunch of other fancy, expensive superhero products out there, but ours was the exact same thing only cheaper. Once the label was designed, the hard part would be thinking up a whole range of products that superheroes just wouldn't be able to live without.*

NOTES: *We discussed for a long time whether or not to include weapons in our line of products. Some of us took the side of Ratgirl, who, for obvious reasons, refuses to even touch a gun unless it's to dismantle it, while others prefer the outlook of Captain Stoplight, who names each of his boomerangs after former girlfriends. At any rate we eventually found these harmless, yet still really fun, "burp guns" that shoot ping-pong balls. The guns quickly became a big hit, so we installed some targets around the store where people can test the gun by trying to shoot the evil super villains, The Respungeants.*

ITEM NUMBER: 826NYC 105
ITEM NAME: High-Pressure Particle Gun
SPECIFICATIONS: 11.25" x 6" x 2.5"
WRITERS: 826NYC team
DESIGNER: Sam Potts
PRICE: $20.00

HIGH-PRESSURE PARTICLE GUN

ITEM NO. 03508

...uns are cast polycarbonate with vibro-urethane treated coating to prevent wear. A ...and-grip pump makes them easy to use, while a positive ion-plated siphon tube makes them ...afe and long lasting. Gun kit comes furnished with six positive-energy particles.

PARTICLE GUN MODEL

...hances efficiency and accuracy to handle ...ler areas than longer rifle models
...ced for over 3000 years of continuous use ...ng SHC approved positive-energy particles)
...erates on 100-150 psi of unfiltered air

ABOUT POSITIVE ENERGY
Positive energy blasting is effective for cleaning, clearing, and stress relieving any subject hardened by exposure to negative energy. Pressure feed guns have less moving parts and require less maintenance than other blast devices, including energy-blasting eyes.

DOMESTIC
UNIT PRICE
(RETAIL)

20.00
PART
PISTOL

BROOKLYN SUPERHERO SUPPLY CO.
DISTRIBUTED BY THE BROOKLYN SUPERHERO SUPPLY CO., BROOKLYN, NY 11215

BROOKLYN SUPERHERO SUPPLY CO.

ITEM NO.
03578

MADE IN U.S.A.

4 IN. RIGID HANDLE STRONG VACUUM SUCTION CUPS

03578 2 04

For flightless sup
Lockable handles cre
vacuum for climbing m

ITEM NUMBER: 826NYC 106
ITEM NAME: 4 Inch Rigid Handle Strong Vacuum Suction Cups
SPECIFICATIONS: 11.75" x 4" x 9"
WRITERS: 826NYC team
DESIGNER: Sam Potts
PRICE: $18.50

NOTES: *It seemed to us that—unless there was some kind of car repair superhero running around—most heroes didn't need to be able to pull dents and dings out of their car. A much cooler way to put suction cups to use is to try and climb up things with them. As an added bonus, watching people come into the store and actually try to climb up the walls with the suction cups helps to keep our store volunteers entertained.*

4IN. STRONG VACUUM SUCTION CUPS (PAIR)

ITEM NO. 03578

One quick stroke on the lockable pumps creates a strong vacuum. Compact, lightweight cups handle heavy lifting of any superheroes encumbered by earth's gravity. Operates best on smooth, nonporous surfaces. Cups are black rubber. Both climbers have red handles.

DOMESTIC
UNIT PRICE
(RETAIL)

18.50
4 INCH
CUPS

ALSO AVAILABLE

Replacement cups. Please ask for ITEM NO.03570 and specify B.S.S.Co. climber cup part number 0003561Z.

WARNING! NEVER EXCEED LOAD CAPACITIES. NEVER USE FOR LIFTING ITEMS THAT HAVE BEEN AFFECTED BY COSMIC RADIATION. NEVER USE WITHOUT PROPER TRAINING OR THE SUPERVISION OF A WARD.

BROOKLYN SUPERHERO SUPPLY CO.

DISTRIBUTED BY THE BROOKLYN SUPERHERO SUPPLY CO., BROOKLYN, NY 11215

NOTES: *The first thing that popped into our heads when we first saw this product was "Hey, that looks like a blob." And I challenge you to think otherwise! See? I thought so. Of course, the second thing that came to us was, "Why would a superhero need to buy a blob?" There really isn't a good answer to that, other than to say that what they really need is the container, so that they have something to store evil blobs in when heroes run across them in their travels. And, finally, "Who would want to buy an empty container?" Thus the Brooklyn Superhero Supply Co. 10oz. Evil Blob Containment Capsule (blob included) was created.*

ITEM NUMBER: 826NYC 107
ITEM NAME: 10oz Evil Blob Containment Capsule
SPECIFICATIONS: 6.25" x 5" x 4.5"
WRITERS: 826NYC team
DESIGNER: Sam Potts
PRICE: $9.99

NOTES: *X-Ray vision has been a staple of the comic book world for a long time, and anyone familiar with old comic books will remember those ads in the back pages for all sorts of crazy products that could be mail-ordered. One item that routinely made appearances was, of course, x-ray glasses. This would eventually lead us to introduce this, the first product in our FantastiCo! line, which displays all of our fantastic(!) but very-cheaply-made superhero accessories.*

ITEM NUMBER: 826NYC 108
ITEM NAME: X-Ray Glasses
SPECIFICATIONS: 6" x 6" x 6"
WRITERS: 826NYC team
DESIGNER: Sam Potts
PRICE: $9.00

NOTES: *Almost every superhero has some kind of secret identity, even if it's not all that secret. And it makes sense; if your job involves intentionally irritating people with superhuman abilities, it's best if they don't know who you really are. With that in mind, we set about mining the internet for pictures of random people whom we could write-up imaginary back-stories about in order to sell as alternate identities. But, how exactly does someone take up a secret identity? We figured, pretty much all you'd need is a sheet to practice your signature, a helpful FAQ, and a handy troubleshooting guide in case of problems. Voila. Just like that, you too can become a white-haired octogenarian who moonlights as Laser Lady, precision-crime fighter. Available in a variety of identities.*

ITEM NUMBER: 826NYC 109
ITEM NAME: Secret Identity Kit
SPECIFICATIONS: 9" x 11.75"
WRITERS: 826NYC team
DESIGNER: Sam Potts
PRICE: $7.99 each

SECRET IDENTITY KIT — SIGNATURE PRACTICE SHEET

INSTRUCTIONS
This form is provided to help you adapt to your new identity. A spontaneous signature is crucial to maintaining a low...

SECRET IDENTITY KIT — LOG OF CONFIDANTS

INSTRUCTIONS
As you use your secret identity, certain situations may require that you take a civilian into your confidence. While it cannot be stressed enough that this should be done as a last resort, you will need to keep a record of those who are aware of your true identity. Keep this log in a secure location!

SECRET IDENTITY KIT — FREQUENTLY ASKED QUESTIONS

"Do I really have to go to work?"

SECRET IDENTITY KIT — EMERGENCY CONTACT INFO

INSTRUCTIONS
While maintaining your secret identity, it may be necessary for authorized personnel to contact you through discretionary channels. Please fill out the form below and return it in secrecy to the Brooklyn Superhero Supply Co.

PROBLEM	SOLUTION
Your nemesis spotted you changing out of your secret identity.	Order a replacement SIK. To prevent this from happening, take the following precautions: Find an easily accessible place to change in, such as a phone booth or dark alley. Try running into the street while you remove your secret identity costume. With luck, you can be in the air before anyone realizes what has happened.

Welcome to the Brooklyn Superhero Supply Co. Secret Identity Kit Program, the premier secret identity program in operation today. No matter how astonishing your superpowers may be, no matter the breadth of your personal charms, a BSS Co. SIK guarantees a virtually impenetrable cloak of mediocrity with every easy-to-operate humdrum guise.

Whether you are:

- Seeking everyday anonymity
- Infiltrating the world of your nemesis
- Just moonlighting for extra cash

with a BSS Co. SIK you'll experience unsurpassed mediocrity and all the security an inauspicious identity can offer.

Exciting upgrades now include Lack-of-Ambition, Social Awkwardness, Political Impotence, Carpal-Tunnel, Low-Grade Depression, Nagging Fear, Self-Sabotage, Yearning, Pudginess, Lactose-Intolerance, and Debt!

While other companies' SIKs can harbor hidden talents, be recognized in unexpected circles, and crash without warning, BSS Co. SIKs are programmed exclusively with the most comprehensive battery of middling quirks and characteristics—guaranteeing coverage so reliably lackluster our SIKs have won the Intergalactic Everyman Award six years running.

Easy to install, low-maintenance, and compatible with most operating systems, our SIKs are designed with your convenience in mind. And all BSS Co. SIK memberships always carry the following privileges:

- Worldwide acceptance at over 14 million locations—your BSS Co. SIK is accepted without question at most U.S. and international establishments including hotels, restaurants, airlines, gas stations, CVS and Rite Aid Pharmacies, dive bars, public transit systems, malls, and government agencies
- 24-hour customer support and on-site emergency troubleshooting, including large-scale mind wipes and port-o-phonebooth placement services
- Replacement programming in the event of irremediable exposure or the unexpected processing of outstanding warrants for arrest
- An inconspicuous and drab tote bag for your convenience (available while supplies last)

At BSS Co. we understand that the power to protect your powers lies in hard-won mediocrity. Thank you for trusting us with your secret identity.

Ever vigilant, ever true,

Cyrus V. Blunt

a

⁴¹Tt
63.25

[Tt] 13²65h⁶07¹
Boiling: 100°C
Melting: 0°C
Density:13°C: 9.9 g/cm²
Ionization at eV: 3

ITEM

time
travel

USES
Allows wearer to move backwards and forwards to different points in time, in a manner analogous to moving through space. May also permit travel between parallel realities.

WARNING
Don't visit yourself in the past.

6% of the proceeds from the sale of this product will be donated on your behalf to The Office of Human Radiation Experiments.

NO. Tt- 8.00

Manufactured in secret.
Conforms to SH-2004 Regulations for energy-related experiments.

Bugayenko Laboratories assumes no responsibility for chemical-burn or experiments gone horribly, horribly wrong.

BUGAYENKO
LABORATORIES
DISTRIBUTED BY THE BROOKLYN SUPERHERO SUPPLY CO.

²⁵**C**

BL-25.9
Boiling: 7˚C
Melting: 22˚C
Density/10˚C
Stability: -4.00

Synthesized in a
controlled environ-
ment far away from
your neighborhood.

chaos

Chaos refers to unpredictability and is
the antithetical concept of cosmos. In
the event of a spill, spill control pillows
can be purchased for absorbing chaos
and other "disorder" related
substances. Spills can also be
neutralized with order.

This product was prepared haphazardly.

5% of the proceeds from the sale of
this product will be donated on your
behalf to The Office of Human
Radiation Experiments.

CH-11.99

Manufactured in secret.
Conforms to SH-2004 Regulations
for time travel-inducing elements.

Bugayenko Laboratories assumes
no responsibility for mutations
or experiments gone horribly,
horribly wrong.

**BUGAYENKO
LABORATORIES**

DISTRIBUTED BY THE BROOKLYN SUPERHERO SUPPLY CO.

b

ITEM NUMBER: a. 826NYC 110,
b. 826NYC 111
ITEM NAME: a. Time Travel, b. Chaos
SPECIFICATIONS: a. 5" x 7.75" x 2"
b. 5" x 9.5" x 3"
WRITERS: 826NYC team
DESIGNER: Sam Potts
PRICE: a. $8, b. $11.99

NOTES: *We had decided fairly early on that we needed to
make room for some kind of strange laboratory products.
After all, not all superheroes were born with their super
powers. Some of them, apparently, bought unreliable
testing materials from a crazy Russian scientist. Part of
the fun of coming up with ideas for this line was knowing
that we wouldn't really be able to explain how these
products were supposed to be used. How exactly does one
apply Time Travel? Orally? Rub it on like lotion? Who
knows? It's still handy to have in an emergency.*

a   b   c

ITEM NUMBER: a. 826NYC 112,
b. 826NYC 113, c. 826NYC 114
ITEM NAME: a. Justice,
b. Mind Control, c. Antidote
SPECIFICATIONS: 5.75" x 2.75" x 2.75"
WRITERS: 826NYC team
DESIGNER: Sam Potts
PRICE: a. $9.99, b. $9.99, c. $9.75

NOTES: *It makes sense that if there's a world of superheroes, there's potentially years of superhero history. And if there's potentially years of superhero history, there's some old guys with beards that did it first. Much like the old elixirs and cure-alls that sham-artists used to sell out of the backs of wagons, we figured that in a world of superheroes, those elixirs might actually work. And so the Aardvark Bros. were born. Seen as kind of pioneers in the field of superhero elixirs, they offer old-timey solutions to combat crime—Justice, Truth Serum, Mind Control, and so on.*

DVARK BROS. STORY

...awn of the Industrial Revolution, the
...ro Chemical Concern Ltd. is the oldest
...erating superhero research and
...mpany in the world today. What began
...small family-owned business in
...Massachusetts, with a
...zation in potent chemical
...ctions to increase
...tude and will power, has
...wn to become the
...ing producer of all
...ner of essential goods
...uperheroes.

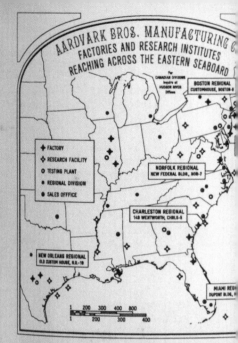

HENRY AARDVARK

...1902, the company was
...from its grand founder,
...h Aaradvark, to his two
...elt and Henry. With a virtuous
...l no small dose of acumen, the brothers
...estigations of their father and expanded
...electro-physics, engineering, mass
...raulics, magnetics, and telekinetic
...nark their broadened range of interests,
...moved to a new remote headquarters in
...n River Valley and officially renamed
...Manufacturing Co. in 1927.

...r, the Aardvark name is respected as the
...ality and ingenuity. Superheroes have
...ed Aardvark products for nearly two
...company has been honored with every
...manufacturing award. At Aardvark,
...dition and innovation builds on a proud
...ment and trust.~~~~~~~~~~

...N USED PROPERLY,
...THIS PRODUCT

—— PROMOTES ——

...ITY, FRESH BREATH,
...F-PRESERVATION,
...CED MOOD SWINGS,
...PROMPTNESS

THIS PRODUCT CONTAINS the finest substances
from exclusive materials. The active ingredien...
product, while secret, include the following prope...

SUBSTANCE	WT. BY VOL.	PER 100
Diabolis	1g	25%
Fat	44Mg	14%
Nasty	0.9g	44%
Paralysis	18g	99%
Protein	59g	55%
Sodium Evil	15g	11%

NOTES: *The Brooklyn and Environs Map was the first poster that we sold, but it didn't actually start out as a poster. We wanted to have a huge, wall-sized map of the five boroughs with helpful information that superheroes could use to combat crime. And so began the incredibly difficult process of creating the map. We not only had to label points of interest all over the map—such as the handy shuttle port located at the top of the Empire State Building—but we also had to figure out a way to hang a gigantic 7' x 6' map on hinges so that we could get behind it for basic maintenance. Eventually we managed to create it and hang it, only to discover that the specialized installation wasn't necessary. Oh well. It still turned out looking pretty good, and spawned a very successful poster.*

ITEM NUMBER: 826NYC 002
ITEM NAME: Brooklyn Poster
SPECIFICATIONS: 24" x 26"
WRITERS: 826NYC team
DESIGNER: Sam Potts
PRICE: $15.00

56

RESIDENTIAL
Beyond the Exosphere is prime space estate zoned for all types of orbiting platforms, satellites, and space stations. This altitude is divided into districts of all sizes, providing spacious quarters for any size organization or league. Special discounts are available for seniors.

EXOSPHERE
Super-height! This altitude is specially zoned for preferred heroes to escape the cares of the Earth's surface. Here, the air is thin yet fragrant, and heroes can relax in the soothing breezes of galactic wind, or visit the surface of any of the convenient orbiting asteroids. Highly accommodating Exospherians are ready to satisfy your every whim.

IONOSPHERE
This zone is reserved for travelling around the globe at supersonic speeds. Heroes may not fly at this altitude at speeds below 3,000,000 mph. Gravity no longer exerts drag on capes and flying is peaceful and dreamy.

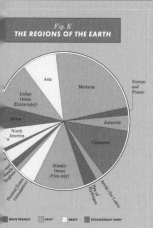

Fig. A
ENJOY ALL THE OUTER ATMOSPHERE HAS TO OFFER!

CHEMOSPHERE
In the Chemosphere, super-vision is required to track movements on the Earth's surface. X-ray vision can still penetrate the Mantle layer (see fig. F). For non-flying heroes, this zone is accessible by orbiters and pods, and features fully staffed rest stops.

STRATOSPHERE
Super-vision is recommended for seeing the dastardly intentions of villains on the Earth's surface. People look like tiny ants. The Stratosphere is the preferred altitude for invisible vehicle travel and sightseeing entire continents.

TROPOSPHERE
The Troposphere is the ideal altitude for patrolling cities and suburbs without the aid of super-vision. Street noises are commonly muffled but cries for help and alert beacons are easily heard.

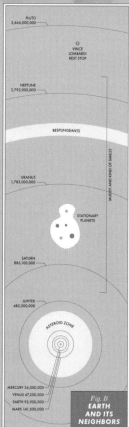

PLUTO
3,666,000,000

VINCE LOMBARDI REST STOP

NEPTUNE
2,793,000,000

RESPUNGEANTS

MUSEUM AND KIND OF SMELLY

STATIONARY PLANETS

URANUS
1,783,000,000

SATURN
886,100,000

JUPITER
483,300,000

ASTEROID ZONE

MERCURY 36,000,000
VENUS 67,200,000
EARTH 92,900,000
MARS 141,500,000

Fig. B
EARTH AND ITS NEIGHBORS

RECOMMENDED "SLINGSHOT" LOCAL PLANETARY TRAVEL WITH (STATIONARY PLANET TO ORBIT)

Fig. C1

HOME PLANET   DESTINAT

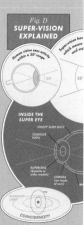

RECOMMENDED FLIGHT FOR INTERPLANETARY T "THE INTERCEPTOR TECH

POSITION AT LAUNCH

HOME PLANET   DESTINAT

Fig. D
SUPER-VISION EXPLAINED

Human vision sees activity within a 20° range

Supervision ha which means and sup

INSIDE THE SUPER EYE

CRUSTY SLEEP DUCT
STUDIOUS PUPIL
SUPERLENS (Eidolin in older models)
CORNEA (for made of ears)

PLANETARY CHILI

COINCIDENCE??

Fig. E
THE REGIONS OF THE EARTH

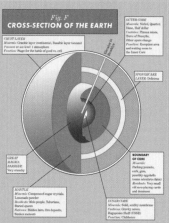

Asia

Mertania

Europe and France

Indian Ocean (Extra spicy)

Africa

Antarctic

North America

Unknown

Atlantic Ocean (Fish only)

Sand of (Less salty)

Arctic (Less salty)

QUITE FRIENDLY   SPICY   GASEY   OCCASIONALLY SHINY

Fig. F
CROSS-SECTION OF THE EARTH

CRUST LAYER
Minerals: Granite layer (continental), Basalt layer (oceanic)
Pressure at sea level: 1 atmosphere
Function: Stage for the battle of good vs. evil

SPONGECAKE LAYER: Deliciousa

OUTER CORE
Minerals: Nickel, Quartez, Dimes, Half dollar
Contains: Plateau mines, Dens of Pennyths, Other spare change
Function: Reception area and waiting room to the Inner Core

GREAT MAGMA BARRIER: Very crunchy

MANTLE
Minerals: Compressed sugar crystals, Lemonade powder
Dissolves: Mole people, Tuberians, Buried spaces
Features: Hidden lairs, Ore deposits, Sunken meteors

BOUNDARY OF CORE
Minerals: Parking pounds, work, gum, possibly eggshells (some scientists claim)
Contains: (very small)
Dissolves: Very small old non-playing cards and dominoes

INNER CODE
Minerals: Solid, scabby membrane
Contains: Gravity mines, Bappendale Shelf (USSE)
Function: Clubhouse

Fig. G2
EARTH TILTED BY ASTRO FORCES

POWERS OF DARKNESS PEEVED OF BRINKLES

NUMBER OF DARKNESS FEELING DISTRIBUTIVE

BROOKLYN FIGHTS BACK

TH FACTS

Memberships:
of Orbiting Moons, of Carbon-Based ms (pending), ntric Association

:
Jupiter, Saturn, nes Pluto

EARTH FACTS

Pressure at Earth's center:
about 3.5 million atmospheres (a lot)

Temperature during really really hot days: 6000–7200°F

Primary Industries:
agriculture, industry, vacations, dastardly plots, foiling, parades

EARTH FACTS

Atmosphere: argon, air, odor, protons, Brooklygen, floaty things, stickiness

Total Surface Area:
196,950,000 square miles (9.7608 x 10^10 large pizzas)

Diameter of the Earth at the Core: 7,927 miles (55,806,080 hot dogs)

EARTH FACTS

Land Area:
57,510,000 square miles

Percentage of land area that's studio apartments: .0056%

Sea Area:
139,440,000 square miles

Drinkable sea area:
36,500 square miles (not including polar ice cubes

EARTH FACTS

Time runs backward:
every 85,000 solar years

Life Forms:
amphibious, invisible, robots, carbon-based, gelatinous, telepathic, rock-based

Formerly classified as:
T-Rock396, Terraball, "Planet Kevin"

a

b

ITEM NUMBER: a. 826NYC 115,
b. 826NYC 116
ITEM NAME: a. Mt. Fortress Tights,
b. Mt. Fortress Cape
SPECIFICATIONS: a. 4" x 3.5"x 3.5",
b. 7" x 6.5" x 6.5"
WRITERS: 826NYC team
DESIGNER: Sam Potts
PRICE: a. $12,
b. $25-$40 (styles vary)

NOTES: *We all knew that the most important aspect of any superhero's repertoire was not his or her gear and gadgets. Oh, no. The single most important thing is the clothing. You could have the coolest gear in the world, but you won't be taken seriously as a hero if you don't wear underwear outside of your tights. And so we had to make sure the label projected a feeling of confidence in our customer that these were indeed the strongest, most rugged and well-tested unitards in the superhero world. We aren't sure whether the clouds or the mountains came first, but in either case, we felt the Mt. Fortress brand exuded the essence of that strength.*

ITEM NUMBER: 826NYC 001

ITEM NAME: BSSC T-shirt

SPECIFICATIONS: 100% cotton

DESIGNER: Sam Potts

PRICE: $15.00

NOTES: *Eventually, everyone sells a T-shirt. They're cheap to make and easy to sell. Ours features our Brooklyn Superhero Supply Co. logo designed by Sam Potts and is offered in a variety of colors. I'm not sure who that is wearing our shirt in the picture, but the dimples do not come with the shirt.*

826MICHIGAN
THE LIBERTY STREET ROBOT SUPPLY & REPAIR

News that yet another robot supply store was opening in downtown Ann Arbor was not well-received. Conventional wisdom suggested that the market was far too small to sustain so many robot-related enterprises in the area, especially in such a sluggish economy. Six months after our grand opening, the critics were proven correct, and we had driven all of our competitors out of business, thereby making Liberty Street Robot Supply & Repair the premier and exclusive destination for all robot enthusiasts in the greater Southeastern Michigan region.

Interior Designers: C. Jason DePasquale, Mollie Edgar, and Amy Sumerton
Window Graphics: Mollie Edgar · *Logo Designer:* Mollie Edgar, mollie-edgar.com
Store Manager: Amy Sumerton
115 EAST LIBERTY STREET, ANN ARBOR, MICHIGAN
WWW.826MICHIGAN.ORG

CLEAN SLATE

CLEAN SLATE

CLEAN SLATE

GLOW

ROBOT LARYNX
(REPLACEMENT)

ROBOT
TOUPEE/
PARTY HAT

ROBOT
TOUPEE/
PARTY HAT

ROBOT
TOUPEE/
PARTY HAT

826MICHIGAN: PROGRAM OVERVIEW

OPENED: June 2005

SERVES: Ann Arbor Public School District, Ypsilanti Public School District, Willow Run Community School District, Lincoln Consolidated School District, and Wayne-Westland Community School District

NEIGHBORHOOD: Ann Arbor

NUMBER OF VOLUNTEERS: 435

MOST RECENT PUBLICATION: *The 826michigan OMNIBUS*—a collection of original writing from seventy 826michigan students between the ages of six and eighteen, containing work from all of 826michigan's programs: tutoring, workshops, in school projects and more, with an introduction (under a pseudonym) by Julie Orringer

IN-SCHOOLS SESSIONS: 152 in 2006–07

WORKSHOPS OFFERED: 64 in 2006-07

TOTAL NUMBER OF STUDENTS SERVED: 1751

TUTORING SPACE: 1,720 square feet

STAFF: Amy Sumerton and Amanda Uhle

Opposite page
ITEM NUMBER: 826MI 100
ITEM NAME: Clean Slate
SPECIFICATIONS: 5.75" x 4.5" x .75"
DESIGNERS: C. Jason DePasquale,
Mollie Edgar, Amy Sumerton
PRICE: $6.00

NOTES: *This was conceived as a low-cost way to reformat your malfunctioning robot's brain. Loosely based on anti-viral software, the gag here relies on understanding that placing a magnet near a computer is a surefire way to erase its hard drive. An unexpected twist: These horseshoe magnets are surprisingly weak. They can barely lift thumb tacks, making our novelty product even more useless than originally intended. The only way to do any real damage with Clean Slate would be to beat it against your computer like a rock.*

ITEM NUMBER: 826MI 101
ITEM NAME: Ultra-Flex
Suspension Coil
SPECIFICATIONS: 11.25" x 2" x 2"
DESIGNERS: C. Jason DePasquale,
Mollie Edgar, Amy Sumerton
PRICE: $5.00

NOTES: *A triumph of the senses: pleasing to the eye on a shelf, fun to shake in the hand (the coil is only fastened at the top, so it compresses and decompresses as you upend it), and the percussive sound that it makes while doing so would serve you well in a community theater production of STOMP. Also, it's made of metal, so if you pop off the lid and lick it, it tastes like a penny. The only sense left unsatisfied is smell, something we'll address in version 2.0.*

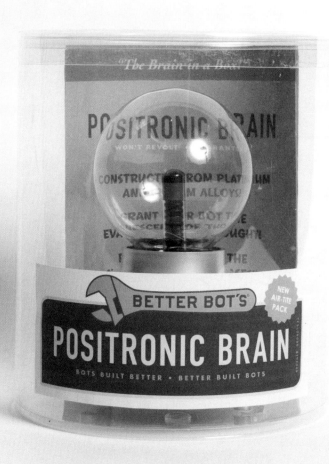

ITEM NUMBER: 826MI 102
ITEM NAME: Positronic Brain
SPECIFICATIONS: 7" x 6" x 6"
DESIGNERS: C. Jason DePasquale, Mollie Edgar, Amy Sumerton
PRICE: $20.00

NOTES: *The term "Positronic Brain" comes from Isaac Asimov by way of Star Trek. In fact, much of our robot-lore comes from Asimov's writing, as filtered through pop culture. For the most part, this has served us well. It's only on the rare occasion that an actual robotics expert wanders into our store that we're forced to confront the fact that we're actually a bunch of frauds and charlatans, making the whole thing up as we go along.*

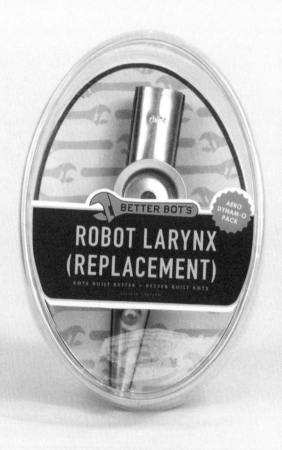

ITEM NUMBER: 826MI 103

ITEM NAME: Robot Larynx (Replacement)

SPECIFICATIONS: 6" x 3.75" x 1.75"

DESIGNERS: C. Jason DePasquale, Mollie Edgar, Amy Sumerton

PRICE: $6.00

NOTES: *"Larynx," as it turns out, is a word that very few people seem to know how to spell or pronounce properly. The correct order of the letters R, Y, and N seems to be a constantly-changing and ultimately-unknowable thing. As a result, this has quietly become our most controversial product.*

ITEM NUMBER: 826MI 104
ITEM NAME: Loose Screws
SPECIFICATIONS: 3.75" x 2.75" x 2.75"
DESIGNERS: C. Jason DePasquale, Mollie Edgar, Amy Sumerton
PRICE: $5.00

NOTES: *This product has the distinction of being the only item in our store that is exactly what it claims to be. Each jar contains a completely random assortment of actual loose screws scavenged from the junk drawers and garages of our volunteers and staff.*

a   b   c

ITEM NUMBER: a. 826MI 105,
b. 826MI 106, c. 826MI 107
ITEM NAME: a. Cough Syrup,
b. On-the-Spot Oil, c. Robot Tears
SPECIFICATIONS: a. 5" x 2" x 1",
b. 4.5" x 1.75" x 1", c. 4.5" x 1" x 1"
DESIGNERS: C. Jason DePasquale,
Mollie Edgar, Amy Sumerton
PRICE: a. $6, b. $5, c. $5

NOTES: *Our customers have a lot of questions about our products. "Why would a robot need tears?" is a common one. The obvious answer: we carry a full line of Emotion Upgrades for your robot, including Sadness, Distress, and Awe, all of which are feelings that are best expressed when accompanied by a stream of tears. This particular trio of products is the closest we come to selling snake oil.*

ITEM NUMBER: 826MI 108
ITEM NAME: By Your Command Bell
SPECIFICATIONS: 3.5" x 3.5" x 2.5"
DESIGNERS: C. Jason DePasquale,
Amy Sumerton
PRICE: $5.00

NOTES: *Amy had always admired these "At Your Service" bells, so she ordered a carton of them and assumed that we would easily come up with a robot-related gimmick for them. Instead, we were stumped for weeks. We finally decided to call them "By Your Command" bells, which is an obscure reference to the 1978 television show* Battlestar Galactica, *just to get them out of our back room. We attached them to red velvet, then packaged them in transparent take-out containers, which further muddied an already confused concept. Inexplicably, they have sold well.*

ITEM NUMBER: 826MI 109
ITEM NAME: Universal Translator
SPECIFICATIONS: 5" x 6" x 2.5"
DESIGNERS: C. Jason DePasquale,
Mollie Edgar, Amy Sumerton
PRICE: $8.00

NOTES: *This voice modulator is a customer favorite. It has three settings: "Robot," "Boy," and "Kid." Marketing a translator as "universal" when it only features three settings is a bold piece of false advertising, made all the more brazen by the fact that "boy" and "kid" would seem to be redundant categories. Nevertheless, this is a big seller.*

ITEM NUMBER: 826MI 110
ITEM NAME: Sushi Buddies
SPECIFICATIONS: 9" x 4.25" x 2"
DESIGNERS: C. Jason DePasquale,
Mollie Edgar, Amy Sumerton
PRICE: $14.00

NOTES: *In the beginning, we conceptualized much of our store over shared meals. At one point, we decided that it would be virtually impossible for a human being to effectively convey the joy of eating a really good sushi roll to his robot companion. In our minds, this was a serious problem, so we created Sushi Buddies as a way to bridge the gap between man and machine. Strangely, what probably should have remained an in-joke between two overtired friends caught on with the general public, and Sushi Buddies has become one of our more beloved products. Includes five wind-up sushi.*

ITEM NUMBER: 826MI 111

ITEM NAME: Beast vs. Machine Action Adventure Set

SPECIFICATIONS: 7" x 3.25" x 3.25"

DESIGNERS: C. Jason DePasquale, Amy Sumerton

PRICE: $8.00

NOTES: *Our epiphanies come late at night. One of them was this: wind-up toys are essentially robots. Both tend to have gears, cogs, and springs, and they both move around. If they're not robots in the proper sense, then they're at least spiritual kin. What seemed like a breakthrough at the time was actually a slippery slope, and soon our store was overrun with wind-up toys. We attempted to justify their presence by packaging them in sets, one of which became The Beast vs. Machine Action Adventure Set, pitting technology's greatest triumph against evolution's biggest failure in a grudge match that spans the ages.*

BEAST VS. MA

CTION-ADVENTUR

- **TITANS CLASH!** A mecha battles one of history's g behemoths!

- **DARWIN AT HOME!** Pit biggest failure against te crowning achievement!

- **BRAINS OR BRAWN?** S timeless debate!

Design by Asimov presents BOT BUDDIES, a full line of gregarious clockwork mechanisms that bridge the gap between human and robot. BOT BUDDIES: amiable affable...Asimov!

pear from the strange land of outsi d be welcomed

ITEM NUMBER: 826MI 112
ITEM NAME: Robot Fashion Bladder
SPECIFICATIONS: 5" x 5" x 5"
DESIGNERS: C. Jason DePasquale,
Amy Sumerton
PRICE: $5.00

NOTES: *A slight miscalculation in measurement during our ordering process yielded a shipment of large bouncing balls, when we had been expecting tiny ones. We put one into the box of a different product to see what it would look like, and were surprised to find that the ball stuck to the top and sides of the package, probably because of science of some sort. "These are... Fashion Bladders," said Amy. "In an... anti-gravity... chamber," added Jason. We quickly packaged them without further discussion and then shamelessly offered them for sale on the shelves of our store.*

NOTES: *On the surface, this is simply a silver piggy bank for your robot. Look deeper and you'll find an art object that asks you to meditate on the concepts of morality, mortality, and the consequences of legacy. You'll also learn a little about compound interest. The thinking behind this product is that while you won't live forever, your properly-maintained robot might. You can reward his faithful service by starting a savings account to sustain him during his lonely eternity without you. This is one of our higher concept products. When we sell it to kids, we generally stick to the "it's a silver piggy bank for your robot" angle.*

ITEM NUMBER: 826MI 113
ITEM NAME: Robot Savings Bank
SPECIFICATIONS: 5" x 5" x 5"
DESIGNERS: C. Jason DePasquale, Mollie Edgar, Amy Sumerton
PRICE: $13.00

ITEM NUMBER: 826MI 114
ITEM NAME: Robot Toupee/Party Hat
SPECIFICATIONS: 13" x 3.5" x 3.5"
DESIGNERS: C. Jason DePasquale,
Mollie Edgar, Amy Sumerton
PRICE: $12.00

NOTES: *Design by Asimov is our line of completely superfluous robot-related items. Form supersedes function, and style trumps all. If there was a robot version of SkyMall catalog, Design by Asimov products would dominate its pages. For example, this fiber optic Toupee/Party Hat glows with a fashionable bluish hue and attaches to your robot's head with "some sort of space-age polymer bonding stuff."*

LIBERTY STREET
ROBOT
SUPPLY & REPAIR
826MICHIGAN

ITEM NUMBER: 826MI 001
ITEM NAME: LSRSR T-shirt
SPECIFICATIONS: 100% cotton
DESIGNER: Mollie Edgar
PRICE: $15.00

NOTES: *Mollie gets sole credit for the logo, and it is gorgeous. We sell about a billion of these each month. The logo also comes on hoodies, tote bags, and stickers.*

826 SEATTLE
THE GREENWOOD SPACE TRAVEL SUPPLY CO.

Greenwood Space Travel Supply is the planet's only purveyor of adventuring necessities, gifts both fine and amusing, objects of distraction, miscellany, and curios defying categorization. Included in our unique collection, one will find scientific theory, fashionable garments suitable for intergalactic diplomatic missions or casual relaxation, tools to remedy any difficulty, companionship, solutions for the difficulties of zero-gravity, and, of course, towels.

All proceeds benefit the writing center, located behind Greenwood Space Travel Supply's functioning Atomic Teleporter.

Window Graphics: Thad Boss, Studio Rayolux · *Video Installation:* Gabe Kean
Interior Designers: Webster Crowell, Paul Hughes, James Addison Smith
Logo Designer: Thad Boss, rayolux.com
Store Manager: Justin Allan
8414 Greenwood Avenue North, Seattle, Washington
www.826Seattle.org

826 SEATTLE: PROGRAM OVERVIEW

OPENED: October 2005

SERVES: Seattle Public School District and
Shoreline Public School District

NEIGHBORHOOD: Greenwood

NUMBER OF VOLUNTEERS: 417

MOST RECENT PUBLICATION: *In the Hood, 52 Short Plays
You Can Perform in Any Place*—written by the students
at Hamilton International Middle School

FIELD TRIPS HOSTED: 57 in 2007–08

IN-SCHOOLS SESSIONS: 88 in 2007–08

WORKSHOPS OFFERED: 36 in 2007–08

TOTAL NUMBER OF STUDENTS SERVED: 1867

TUTORING SPACE: 1,930 square feet

STAFF: Samar Abulhassan, Justin Allan, Alex Allred, Teri Hein,
Toffer Lehnherr, Yoko Ott, and Devyn Perez

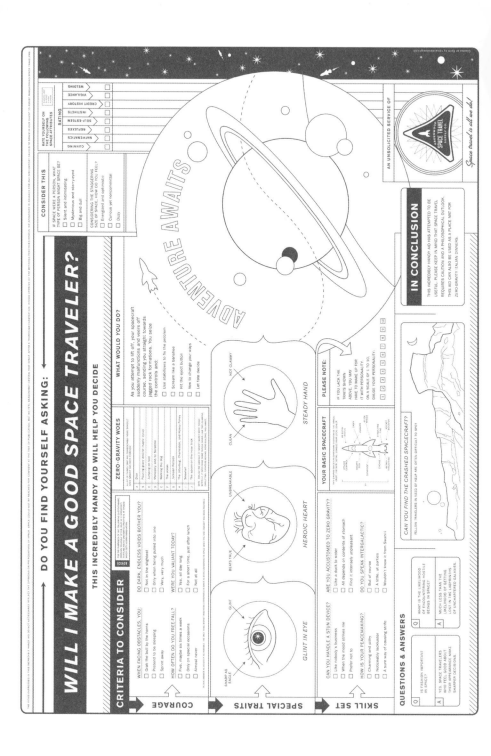

ZERO-GRAVITY WOES

LIST OF THINGS THAT ARE CONSIDERABLY MORE DIFFICULT
[ON]CE GRAVITY HAS BEEN REMOVED:

Dice
Pouring gravy and/or maple syrup
Jumping on bed
Monopoly and/or Scrabble
Walking the dog
The ocean
Jackson Pollock
The Jitterbug, Charleston, and Hokey Pokey
Snowfall
The spoon-on-the-nose trick

[NO]TE: THOUGH THE ABSENCE OF GRAVITY MAKES MANY THINGS
[DIF]FICULT, IT DOES MAKE SOME THINGS EASIER, LIKE TREE-CLIMBING,
[CAR]-LIFTING, FURNITURE-MOVING, ROME-BUILDING, AND KARATE.

WHAT W

As you attempt to li
suddenly malfunctic
course, sending you
jagged rock formati
the controls and:

☐ Use stabilizers to f

☐ Scream like a bans

☐ Hit the eject buttor

☐ Vow to change you

☐ Let fate decide

[BRE]AKABLE   CLEAN   NOT CLAMM[Y]

detail

ITEM NUMBER: 826SEA 1005
ITEM NAME: Space Traveler Poster
SPECIFICATIONS: 18" x 24"
WRITER/DESIGNER: Tim Sanders
PRICE: $10.00

NOTES: *We often find that terrestrial dwellers are unsure
if they possess the skills necessary for travel into space.
This handy guide tests basic knowledge of the universe,
lists clearly the special characteristics common to adept
journeyers, and leads aspiring astronauts on an
introspective journey. This is a very popular and
useful item.*

a

Creating a singularity has never been so easy.

Often regarded as the most horrifying force in the universe, the super concentrated gravity of the black hole is not only useful for jump-starting the spiral motion of a galaxy, it is also an ideal catalyst for generating worm holes to aid in long-distance interstellar space and/or time travel. Compressed molecular empty space and distorted time trajectories are worries of the past with this easy-to-use Black Hole Starter Kit.

Warning: Incorrect use of a black hole may cause widespread destruction, creation of recurrent time-loop anomalies, and an unpleasant buzzing sound.

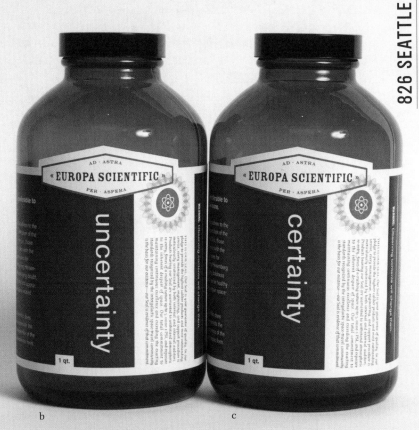

b c

ITEM NUMBER: a. 826SEA 5001,
b. 826SEA 5016, c. 826SEA 5015
ITEM NAME: a. Black Hole Starter Kit,
b. Uncertainty, c. Certainty
SPECIFICATIONS: a. 5" x 4.25" x 4.25",
b. 7" x 3.5" x 3.5", c. 7" x 3.5" x 3.5"
WRITERS: Justin Allan,
Bethany Jean Clement, Paul Hughes
DESIGNER: Thad Boss, Studio Rayolux
PRICE: a. $8, b. $9, c. $9

NOTES: *The more we learn about science (particularly microcosmic space and theoretic physics), the more we appreciate the majesty of outer space; the mysteries of even the smallest elements answer questions about the largest celestial bodies and most fundamental qualities of the universe. The entire line of Europa Scientific products appeals to customers for precisely the same reason.*

ITEM NUMBER: 826SEA 1051

ITEM NAME: Cherry Scented Diversion Deployment System

SPECIFICATIONS: 12" x 12" x 4.25"

WRITER: Bethany Jean Clement

DESIGNER: Julia-Anne Endicott Bork

PRICE: $25.00

NOTES: *The Cherry Scented Diversion Deployment System is one of my favorite product packages; it perfectly encapsulates the early 20th century design, primitive printing production techniques, and overly verbose aesthetic typical of our product line.*
—Justin Allan

DECORATIVE
ENGAGING
PURPOSIVE
USABLE
PRACTICABLE
RED

PANIC BUTTON

ITEM NUMBER: 826SEA 1043
ITEM NAME: Panic Button
SPECIFICATIONS: 4" x 4" x 4"
WRITER: Justin Allan
DESIGNER: Julia-Anne Endicott Bork
PRICE: $6.00

NOTES: *The Panic Industries line of products (necessities for emergency situations—analog alarms, lights, and navigation systems, spare cans of emergency jet fuel) was one of the first product lines I conceived. It went through several unsuccessful incarnations before it was handed to Julia. I showed her a* Collier's *magazine cover from WWII designed by Lester Beall, said "make it look like that," and within two days, Julia had created one of our most iconographic product lines. —Justin Allan*

OUR MISSION:

SnackTime's mission in its entirety is to make snacking universally practicable and optimally satisfying.

Snackers who aren't themselves snacking professionals require a quality vendor of reliable snackware, snack service, and snack support. SnackTime is such a vendor. We serve our clients as a trusted ally, providing them with the loyalty of a partner in snack-related endeavors in our role as vendor. We seek to ensure that our clients have what they need to enjoy their snacking to the fullest possible extent, with maximum efficiency and reliability. Many of our snacking applications are certified as mission critical, with said certifications available for review through the relevant governing bodies. When our clients need us—no matter how extraordinary or routine the circumstances—they have the assurance that we will be there.

SnackTime is committed to being the "Supplier of Choice" for snack-related paraphernalia through product and service excellence. Our emphasis is on being a responsible, innovative snacking partner providing value-added, real-time services to our customers and suppliers worldwide. Your satisfaction in snacking is our number-one goal, while simultaneously we seek to uphold our long-held tradition of commitment to snack service, ethical snacking practices, and general equanimity.

SnackTime's utility and ease of use have made it one of the world's best-known brands, almost entirely through word of mouth from satisfied users. We thank you for your loyalty, and we wish

ITEM NUMBER: 826SEA 4053
ITEM NAME: Zero-Gravity Spaghetti Containment Device
SPECIFICATIONS: 13" x 2.5" x 2.5"
TEMPLATE DESIGNER: Laura Williams
WRITER/DESIGNER: Paul Barrett
PRICE: $12.00

NOTES: *Last time I was floating about in high orbit around Neptune, I found myself with a conundrum; I had just picked out some excellent take-out from Neptune Nepoli, but due to the lack of gravity, I was having a terrible time wrangling the fettuccine alfredo without making an absolute mess. What I—and every space traveler— desperately needed was a tool to keep the noodles properly contained. Thus, the Zero-Gravity Spaghetti Containment Device.*

ITEM NUMBER: 826SEA 1064
ITEM NAME: Near-Death Ray
SPECIFICATIONS: 8.5" x 11.75" x 2"
WRITER: Bethany Jean Clement
DESIGNER: Thad Boss, Studio Rayolux
PRICE: $6.00

NOTES: *Why kill when you can be stunning?*
Enough said.

ASSEMBLY INSTRUCTIONS

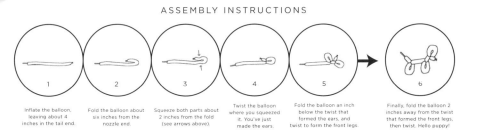

1. Inflate the balloon, leaving about 4 inches in the tail end.

2. Fold the balloon about six inches from the nozzle end.

3. Squeeze both parts about 2 inches from the fold (see arrows above).

4. Twist the balloon where you squeezed it. You've just made the ears.

5. Fold the balloon an inch below the twist that formed the ears, and twist to form the front legs.

6. Finally, fold the balloon 2 inches away from the twist that formed the front legs, then twist. Hello puppy!

ITEM NUMBER: 826SEA 1033
ITEM NAME: Planetary Puppy
SPECIFICATIONS: 5" x 7.5"
WRITER/DESIGNER: Tim Sanders
PRICE: $2.00

NOTES: *While on long interstellar journeys, humans need companionship, but need to always be wary of the amount of cargo and number of passengers. The Planetary Puppy is the ideal answer to both of these conundrums as it is compact, easy to stow, and companionable.*
Includes instruction postcard and two balloons in airtight container.

SIC ITUR
AD ASTRA

li'l BABY
SPUTNIK

Tested by babies—trusted by adventurers.

LI'L TRAVELING UNIFORM

As any experienced traveler can tell you, a versatile, resilient, and stylish outfit is a necessary provision on any sortie — be it into the far reaches of space or simply around the block. The Li'l Baby Sputnik brand Li'l Traveling Uniform is a perfect addition to the wardrobe of any small humanoid. Avoid the embarrassment of being caught unclothed, and confidently wear an outfit that is comfortable and fashionable.

ALL-IN-ONE!
NO PARTS TO LEAVE BEHIND

SOOTHING
COLOR WILL IMPRESS AND ASTONISH

EASY TO SOIL, EASY TO WASH

DISTRIBUTED BY THE
GREENWOOD SPACE TRAVEL SUPPLY Co
SEATTLE, WASHINGTON, USA, EARTH, SOL, VIA LACTEA
WWW.GREENWOODSPACETRAVELSUPPLY.COM

a - tag

SIC ITUR
AD ASTRA

THUS ONE GOES TO THE STARS

The launch and three-month orbit of Sputnik 1 — the first man-made orbiting satellite — in 1957 marked mankind's first baby step into space. An astonished populace was offered a new, tantalizing peek into the starry expanse, amazed by the limitless possibilities. A vast breadth of new experiences, daring adventures, and thrilling discoveries could be envisioned from the trajectory of the small, beeping sphere. The universe was once again new and exciting.

SPUTNIK IS A RUSSIAN WORD MEANING "TRAVELING COMPANION" OR "SATELLITE."

All proceeds from the sale of this item, and items like it, benefit 826 Seattle, a not-for-profit writing and tutoring center for students ages 6 to 18. For more information, visit www.826seattle.org

b - tag

ITEM NUMBER: a. 826SEA 1203,
b. 826SEA 1202
ITEM NAME: a. Li'l Traveling Uniform,
b. Li'l Traveling Wrap
SPECIFICATIONS: a. varies, b. 34" x 34"
WRITER: Justin Allan
TAG DESIGNER: Katie Pickard
DESIGNER: Julia-Anne Endicott Bork
PRICE: $20.00 each

NOTES: *After the birth of two 826 Seattle babies, it became apparent that we were in need of infant-wear. What better to represent the start of a new life than the start of space exploration (the launch of the Sputnik satellite on October 4th, 1957)?*

a

b

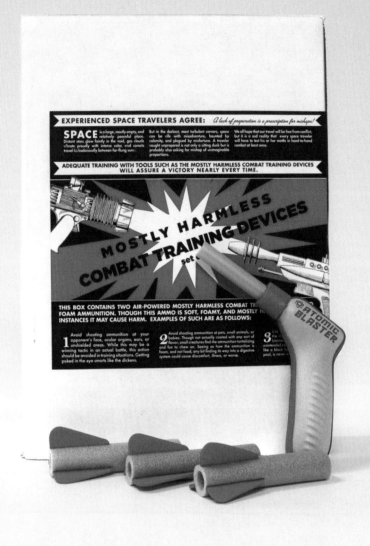

ITEM NUMBER: 826SEA 1050
ITEM NAME: Mostly Harmless Combat Training Devices
SPECIFICATIONS: 9.5" x 13" x 2.25"
WRITER/DESIGNER: Justin Allan
PRICE: $10.00

NOTES: *In space, there are troubles and tribulations innumerable. Space travelers of all stripes have to be prepared, and there is no classier defense than a classically styled ray gun. There is a fine line when it comes to selling weapons and weapon simulators in a youth oriented environment, and it was with that in mind that we designed the Mostly Harmless Combat Training Devices. It is best to be prepared, but to do so safely.*

SPACE VEHICLE HULL REPAIR PATCH

FOR EMERGENCY USE ONLY

TO ADDRESS THE DANGER AND EMBARRASSMENT ASSOCIATED WITH VIOLENT DECOMPRESSION

WARNING: This patch cannot repair massive structural failure. For interplanetary travel only. Not appropriate for atmospheric, interstellar, and/or faster-than-light use. Do not exceed 30,000 km/s or expose patch to unreasonable expectations. Universal Mishap Patent Pending with Marshall Manufacturing. Distributed on Earth by Greenwood Space Travel Supply Co.

ITEM NUMBER: 826SEA 1025
ITEM NAME: Space Vehicle
Hull Repair Patch (magnet)
SPECIFICATIONS: 3.5" x 3.5"
WRITER: Paul Hughes
DESIGNER: Thad Boss, Studio Rayolux
PRICE: $3.00

NOTES: *We find it is always best to be prepared, even against the smallest perturbations. Quickly patching a hole in your hull is a skill with which every traveler should be equipped.*

EXPERIENCED SPACE TRAVELERS AGREE:

A LACK OF PREPARATION IS A PRESCRIPTION FOR MISHAPS.

GREENWOOD SPACE TRAVEL SUPPLY CO

8414 GREENWOOD AVE N
SEATTLE WA 98103

206.725.2625

ALSO HOME OF

826
SEATTLE

ALSO HOME OF

826
SEATTLE

ITEM NUMBER: 826SEA 1092
ITEM NAME: Bumper Sticker
SPECIFICATIONS: 3" x 12"
WRITERS: Paul Hughes, Bethany Jean Clement
DESIGNER: Justin Allan
PRICE: $3.00

EXPERIENCED SPACE TRAVELERS AGREE: A LACK OF PREPARATION IS A PRESCRIPTION FOR MISHAPS.

GREENWOOD
SPACE TRAVEL
SUPPLY CO.

ITEM NUMBER: 826SEA 3023
ITEM NAME: Humanoid
Soft Fiber Garment
SPECIFICATIONS: 100% cotton
LOGO DESIGNER: Thad Boss, Studio Rayolux
T-SHIRT DESIGNER: Donica Ida
PRICE: $20.00

NOTES: *We find that being well-dressed is important, particularly when meeting interstellar dignitaries.*

826LA
THE ECHO PARK TIME TRAVEL MART

The Echo Park Time Travel Mart is the world's leader in convenience retailing for time travelers. We have branches in most time periods, from the Big Bang to the Omega Point. With warp drives, chain mail, and snacks, snacks, snacks, we sell everything you need for a road trip through the fourth dimension. Be sure to visit our newest store, in Los Angeles, which is open from January, 2007 until March, 2482. Remember: Whenever you are, we're already then.

THE ECHO PARK TIME TRAVEL MART

Architect: R. Scott Mitchell · *Interior Designers:* Mac Barnett, Stefan G. Bucher, R. Scott Mitchell
Logo Designer: Stefan G. Bucher, 344design.com
Store Manager: Christina Galante
826LA East, 1714 West Sunset Boulevard, Echo Park, California
826LA West, 685 Venice Boulevard, Venice, California
www.826LA.org

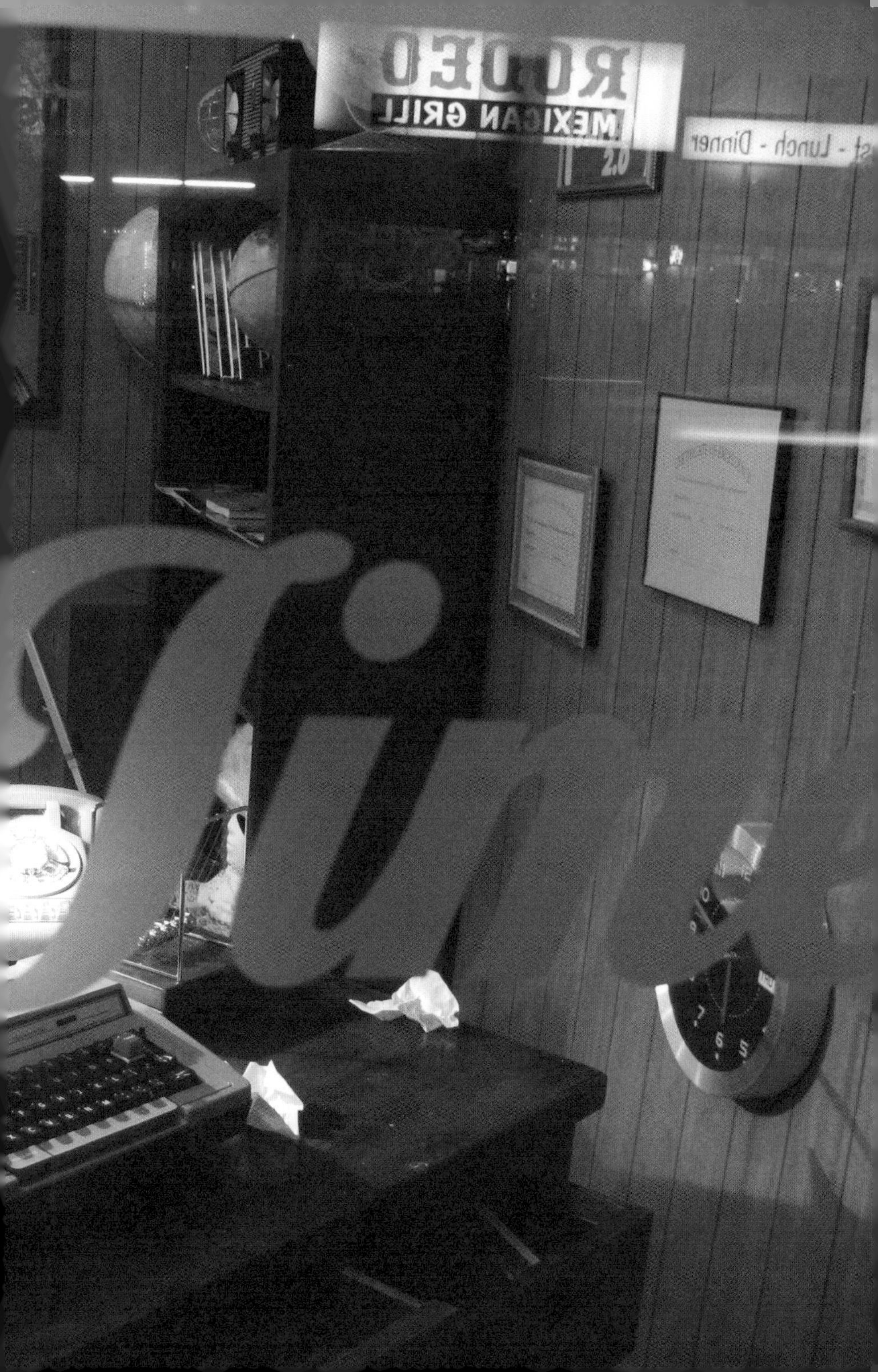
RODEO
MEXICAN GRILL
st - Lunch - Dinner

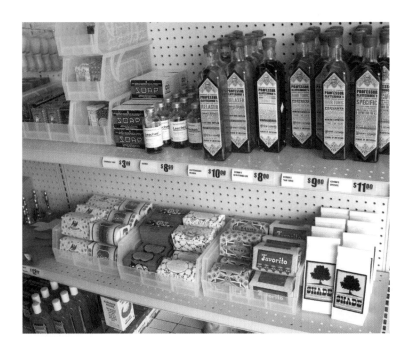

826LA: PROGRAM OVERVIEW

OPENED: March 2005

SERVES: Los Angeles Unified School District

NEIGHBORHOODS: Venice and Echo Park

NUMBER OF VOLUNTEERS: 1180

MOST RECENT PUBLICATION: *Sheep Can't Fly*—a collection of stories on the hero's journey by students at Garfield High School

FIELD TRIPS HOSTED: 25 in 2007–08

IN-SCHOOLS SESSIONS: 129 in 2007–08

WORKSHOPS OFFERED: 30 in 2007–08

TOTAL NUMBER OF STUDENTS SERVED: 1,785

TUTORING SPACE: 3,450 square feet

STAFF: Joel Arquillos, Bonnie Chau, Christina Galante, Danny Hom, and Julius Diaz Panoriñgan

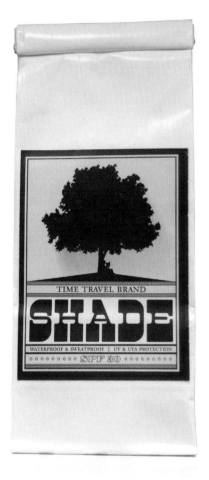

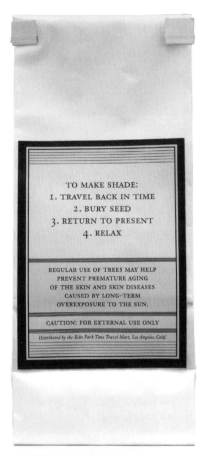

TIME TRAVEL BRAND

SHADE

WATERPROOF & SWEATPROOF | UV & UVA PROTECTION

SPF 30

TO MAKE SHADE:
1. TRAVEL BACK IN TIME
2. BURY SEED
3. RETURN TO PRESENT
4. RELAX

REGULAR USE OF TREES MAY HELP
PREVENT PREMATURE AGING
OF THE SKIN AND SKIN DISEASES
CAUSED BY LONG-TERM
OVEREXPOSURE TO THE SUN.

CAUTION: FOR EXTERNAL USE ONLY

Distributed by the Echo Park Time Travel Mart, Los Angeles, Calif.

ITEM NUMBER: 826LA 100
ITEM NAME: Shade
SPECIFICATIONS: 3.5" x 7.75" x 2.5"
WRITERS: Mac Barnett, Jon Korn
DESIGNER: Stefan G. Bucher, 344 Design
PRICE: $7.99

NOTES: *Developed by botanists and dermatologists, Shade is a great way to protect your skin from the harmful rays of the sun. To use Shade, simply travel back in time, bury the bag in fertile soil, then return to the present. Best of all, Shade is all natural. (Warning: Improper use of Shade may result in splinters.)*

ITEM NUMBER: 826LA 101
ITEM NAME: Caveman Candy
SPECIFICATIONS: 10.5" x 4.75"
WRITERS: Mac Barnett, Jon Korn
DESIGNER: Stefan G. Bucher, 344 Design
PRICE: $4.99

NOTES: *Gamey and tart, every bite of Caveman Candy is bursting with the flavor of prehistoric cave bears. Not only does it satisfy cavemen's chewing needs, but it also keeps their gums healthy and removes tartar. (Some cavemen were harmed in the making of this product.)*

a

b

NOTES: *Mssrs. Smith & Smythe are renowned throughout the colonies as Anglicisers sans pareil and purveyors of the Most English Things on Earth. Our exclusive line of essentially English victuals and supplies are used with pride by the Royal Navy, Her Majesty's Grenadier Highlanders, and the Ministry of Science, Naturalists and Manners. Smith & Smythe's upper-lip stiffening English inventions include Curry, Gunpowder, and Tea. The Sun Never Sets on Us!*

ITEM NUMBER: a. 826LA 102, b. 826LA 103
ITEM NAME: a. Pure English Gunpowder,
b. Pure English Curry
SPECIFICATIONS: 11" x 6.5" x 4.5"
WRITERS: Mac Barnett, Jon Korn
DESIGNER: Stefan G. Bucher, 344 Design
PRICE: a. $6.99, b. $6.99

Smith & Smythe

PURE ENGLISH GUNPOWDER IN TRAVEL-SIZED BAG
The Wandering Englishman's Favorite Companion

—— IS IT NOT REMARKABLE? ——
WHEN COMBINED WITH ENGLISH GUNPOWDER,
THESE FACTS ARE SURE TO IMPRESS EVEN THE MOST SKEPTICAL FOREIGNERS.

The English are the most industrious People on the face of the Earth.
A single ten-year-old English girl does the work of three grown American men.

A recent survey conducted by the Royal Navy (the world's leading consumer
of English Gunpowder) found that well over 99% of people 'wish they were British.'

The English invented French Kissing.

All the best writers are English. In fact, Oscar Wilde, Jonathan Swift, and Dante Alighieri
all attended the same grammar school in Sussex.

Ingredients: Sulfur, Magick, Infernium, Artificial Flavours and Colours.

Attention must be paid: PLEASE KEEP ENGLISH GUNPOWDER OUT OF THE HANDS OF COLONISTS.

Distributed in This and adjoining Time Periods by the Echo Park Time Travel Mart, Los Angeles, Calif., U.S.A.

ITEM NUMBER: 826LA 104
ITEM NAME: Leeches
SPECIFICATIONS: 5" x 1.75" x 1.75"
WRITERS: Mac Barnett, Jon Korn
DESIGNER: Stefan G. Bucher, 344 Design
PRICE: $8.99   NOTES: *Nature's tiny doctors.*

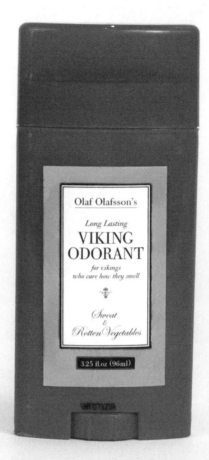

ITEM NUMBER: 826LA 105

ITEM NAME: Viking Odorant

SPECIFICATIONS: 5.75" x 2.5"

WRITERS: Mac Barnett, Jon Korn

DESIGNER: Stefan G. Bucher, 344 Design

PRICE: $6.99

NOTES: *Real Viking Stench for Real Vikings. Olaf Olaffson's Viking Odorant comes in four scents: Toenails, Pyre Ash, Sweat & Rotten Vegetables, and Cod. Because "Axe Body Spray" is something you should find on the battlefield, not under your arms.*

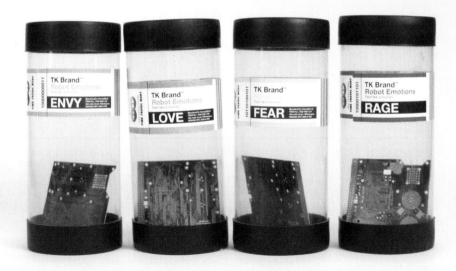

TK Brand™
Robot Emotions
Feel like a human.

FEAR

ITEM NUMBER: 826LA 106
ITEM NAME: Robot Emotions
SPECIFICATIONS: 9" x 4" x 4"
WRITERS: Mac Barnett, Jon Korn
DESIGNER: Stefan G. Bucher, 344 Design
PRICE: $14.99 each

NOTES: *These premium emotion-upgrade chips allow a robot to feel like a human. Available in nine classic emotions: Happiness, Love, Gratitude, Guilt, Schadenfreude, Rage, Envy, Fear and Boredom. 100% not organic.*

a   b

ITEM NUMBER: a. 826LA 107, b. 826LA 108
ITEM NAME: a. Dead Languages: Latin
b. Dead Languages: Coptic
SPECIFICATIONS: 8.5" x 3.5" x 3.5"
WRITERS: Mac Barnett, Jon Korn
DESIGNER: Stefan G. Bucher, 344 Design
PRICE: $8.99 each

NOTES: *Bottled at the source, our exclusive line of Dead Languages still sound as fresh as the day they were spoken. You've already mastered your mother tongue—now get to know your weird-uncle tongues. Available in Latin, Rongorongo, Ancient Greek, Coptic, Sanskrit, Ancient Egyptian, and Delaware.*

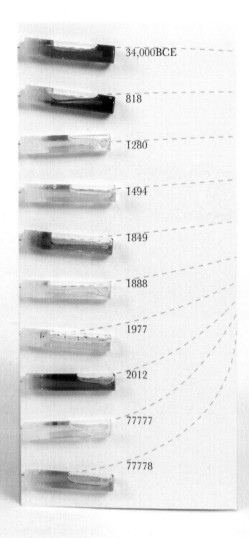

34,000BCE

818

1280

1494

1849

1888

1977

2012

77777

77778

ITEM NUMBER: 826LA 109
ITEM NAME: Timeline of Fragrances
SPECIFICATIONS: 8.5" x 4"
FRAGRANCE DESIGNER: Yosh Han
WRITERS: Mac Barnett, Jon Korn
DESIGNER: Christina Galante
PRICE: Full line of ten 1ml vials $49.99

NOTES: *Created exclusively for The Echo Park Time Travel Mart, we have ten amazing fragrances to choose from—for whenever you need to smell your best. Also available as individual 5ml bottles for $24.99*

Most of civilization's biggest discoveries can be attributed to a specific person.
WHY NOT GO BACK IN TIME AND TAKE CREDIT FOR THE FEW THAT ARE LEFT?

TO ACT LIKE YOU INVENTED FIRE

 GO WHEN: **790,001 B.C.**
WHERE: **SOUTHERN AFRICA**

USE FIRE **AT HOME:**

USE FIRE **AT WORK:**

OR WITH YOUR **FAMILY:**

CONTENTS: **FIRE**

ITEM NUMBER: 826LA 110
ITEM NAME: Ah-Ha Fire
SPECIFICATIONS: 6.25" x 7.5" x 6.25"
WRITERS: Mac Barnett, Jon Korn
DESIGNER: Stefan G. Bucher, 344 Design
PRICE: $19.99

NOTES: *Many of civilization's most important discoveries can be attributed to a specific person. So for the few that are left unclaimed, why not take credit? The Ah-Ha line of products allows time travelers to return to the past and reinvent themselves as inventors. 98% of our customers report being hailed as geniuses and even gods, with less than 2% being tried for witchcraft.*

ITEM NUMBER: 826LA 111
ITEM NAME: Ah-Ha Perspective
SPECIFICATIONS: 3" x 5.75" x 3"
WRITERS: Mac Barnett, Jon Korn
DESIGNER: Stefan G. Bucher, 344 Design
PRICE: $7.99

NOTES: *Add a new dimension to your art with Ah-Ha Perspective.*

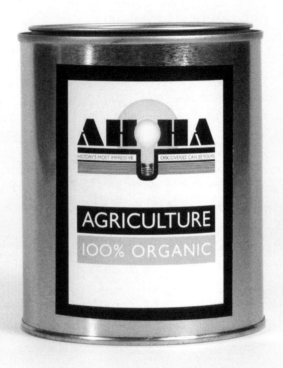

ITEM NUMBER: 826LA 112
ITEM NAME: Ah-Ha Agriculture
SPECIFICATIONS: 5" x 4" x 4"
WRITERS: Mac Barnett, Jon Korn
DESIGNER: Stefan G. Bucher, 344 Design
PRICE: $12.99

NOTES: *In just twelve easy steps, you can transform a bunch of nomads into a Genuine Agrarian Community. Ah-Ha Agriculture contains soil and seeds inside an attractive growing tin, and so may be subject to seizure at certain inter-temporal custom points.*

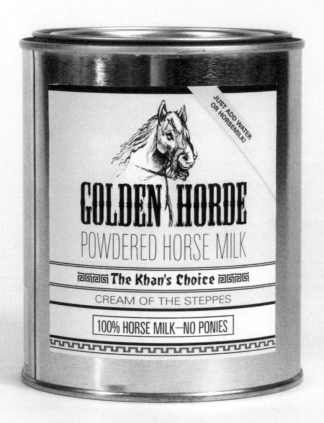

ITEM NUMBER: 826LA 113
ITEM NAME: Powdered Horse Milk
SPECIFICATIONS: 5" x 4.25" x 4.25"
WRITERS: Mac Barnett, Jon Korn
DESIGNER: Stefan G. Bucher, 344 Design
PRICE: $5.99

NOTES: *From our yurt to yours, this Mongol favorite is an ideal drink for both seasons. Just add water or horse milk. Recipes included.*

Nutrition Facts

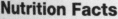

Serving Size 1 can (480g)
Servings Per Container 1

Amount Per Serving	
Calories 3328	Calories from Fat 1900

	%Daily Value*
Total Fat 212g	326%
Saturated Fat 200g	308%
Cholesterol 900mg	300%
Sodium 2,400mg	100%
Total Carbohydrate 300g	100%
Dietary Fiber 25g	100%
Sugars 36g	100%
Protein 55g	

Vitamin A 2%	•	Vitamin C 4%
Calcium 110%	•	Iron 0%

Percent Daily Values are based on a 2,000 calorie diet. Your daily values may be higher or lower depending on your calorie needs.

Calories		2,000	2,500
Total Fat	Less than	65g	80g
* Sat Fat	Less than	20g	25g
Cholesterol	Less than	300mg	300mg
Sodium	Less than	2,400mg	2,400mg
Total Carbohydrate		300g	375g
Dietary Fiber		25g	30g

Calories per gram:
Fat 9 • Carbohydrate 4 • Protein 4

TRY THESE GREAT RECIPES!

HORSE MILK HOT CHOCOLATE
PERFECT FOR SIEGES

Mix 4 spoonfuls Golden Horde Powdered Horse Milk with 1 quart of water or horse milk. Add chocolate to taste. Boil until chunky.

HORSE MILK BLONDIES
DEZUNGAR'S FAVORITE

Mix ½ cup of Golden Horde Powdered Horse Milk with 1 cup of water or horse milk. Add ½ cup flour, 1 teaspoon sugar, and ½ pound horse butter. Pour mixture into pan and cook over open flame until Blondies are golden brown or you are overwhelmed by the stench of horse milk.

Distributed exclusively
by Echo Park Time Travel Mart
Los Angeles, California

NOTES: *At Jupiter Farms, we still do things the old-fashioned way. We milk our robots by hand, then irradiate the product with pulse lasers to remove molecular impurities. We're a small, family-run farm. Our 80,000 robots are kept in a vast, windowless building, carefully heated to 800 Kelvins for maximum efficiency—and creamy taste. That's the way we've always done it. And it's the way we always will.*

a   b   c

ITEM NUMBER: a. 826LA 115, b. 826LA 116, c. 826LA 117
ITEM NAME: a. Relaxer, b. Hair Tonic, c. Specific
SPECIFICATIONS: 10.5" x 2.25" x 2.25"
DESIGNER: Stefan G. Bucher, 344 Design
PRICE: a. $10, b. $9, c. $11

NOTES: *Professor Constantine Q. Clutterbuck A.M., M.D., LL.D., F.R.M.F., toils Hercules-like in his marvelous scientific laboratory, never wavering from his aim to relieve humankind of their every ache, pain, and prickle. To this date, his patented nostrums and panaceas have delivered more than a million souls from the foul privations of bodily frailty and mental collapse. Says satisfied customer General H.K. Timurline, "Truly this Clutterbuck is some kind of chemical magus! Three cheers for Clutterbuck, and five for his miraculous tonics!"*

133

ITEM NUMBER: 826LA 118
ITEM NAME: Mug
SPECIFICATIONS: 3.75" x 3" x 3"
DESIGNER: Stefan G. Bucher, 344 Design
CONCEPT: Christina Galante
PRICE: $5.99

NOTES: *Show your support for the largest corporation of all time with our exclusive line of logoware and travel gear. The Echo Park Time Travel Mart is the leader in convenience retailing for time travelers. With locations in every time, we're always then when you need us.*

a

b

c

ITEM NUMBER: a. 826LA 119, b. 826LA 120, c. 826LA 121
ITEM NAME: a. Pin, b. Key Chain, c. Luggage Tag
SPECIFICATIONS: a. 1" x 1", b. 1.5" x 1.5", c. 4.25" x 2.25"
DESIGNER: Stefan G. Bucher, 344 Design
CONCEPT: Christina Galante
PRICE: a. $0.99, b. $3.99, c. $3.99

a

b

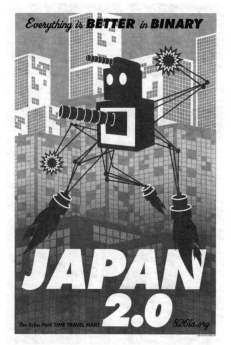

c

d

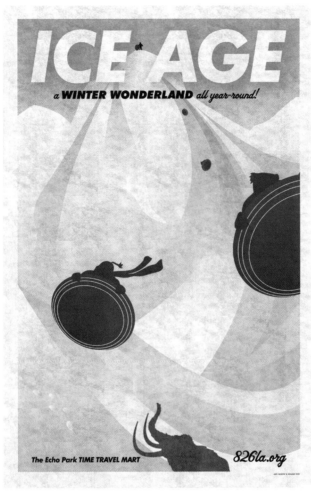

e

ITEM NUMBER: a. 826LA 200, b. 826LA 201,
c. 826LA 202, d. 826LA 203, e. 826LA 204
ITEM NAME: a. In Space Poster,
b. Feudal Japan Poster, c. Japan 2.0 Poster,
d. Pangaea Poster, e. Ice Age Poster
SPECIFICATIONS: 18" x 27"
WRITERS: Mac Barnett, Jon Korn
DESIGNER: Amy Martin
PRICE: $19.99 each, $89.99 for all five

NOTES: *Our beautiful posters from the
golden age of time travel are the next best
thing to being then.*

ITEM NUMBER: a. 826LA 002, b. 826LA 003
ITEM NAME: a. Future Adult T-shirt, b. Onesie
SPECIFICATIONS: 100% cotton
DESIGNER: Stefan G. Bucher, 344 Design
CONCEPT: Mac Barnett, Christina Galante, Jon Korn
PRICE: a. $15.99, b. $15.99

NOTES: *This green shirt is designed for children. It will also fit super intelligent chimps, although the joke doesn't work as well. As for the onesie, everybody knows babies love time travel.*

ITEM NUMBER: 826LA 001
ITEM NAME: T-shirt
SPECIFICATIONS: 100% cotton
DESIGNER: Stefan G. Bucher, 344 Design
CONCEPT: Mac Barnett, Jon Korn
PRICE: $15.99

NOTES: *This t-shirt depicts "The Handshake," commemorating the historic peace treaty between cavemen and robots.*

BIGFOOT
826
BOSTON
3035
BIGFOOT RESEA ARCH INSTITUTE
GREATER BOSTON

826 BOSTON
THE GREATER BOSTON BIGFOOT RESEARCH INSTITUTE

The Greater Boston Bigfoot Research Institute (GBBRI) dedicates itself to furthering the cryptozoological sciences. Located in Roxbury's Egleston Square, GBBRI hosted the North American Sasquatch Symposium in 2007 and houses the Simulactron, the world's only climate simulation chamber for alpine explorers. GBBRI offers bi-weekly seminars such as *Semaphore*, *Language Centers of the Sasquatch Brain*, and *Safe Stunning and Netting Methods*. Its lofty mission concludes, "Let our research be not a bright light but a burning torch in the hands of those who align themselves with our worthy mission."

We exist because he exists

Architects: Geoff Hackett, Ned Hackett, Matt Payette, Jon Racek, Other City Builders
Interior Designer: Megan Dickerson · *Creative Director:* Daniel Johnson
Graphic Designer: Amanda McCorkle, colorquarry.com
Store Manager: Daniel Johnson
3035 Washington Street, Roxbury, Massachusetts
www.826Boston.org

826 BOSTON: PROGRAM OVERVIEW

OPENED: September 2007

SERVES: Boston Public School District and greater Boston area school districts

NEIGHBORHOOD: Egleston Square, Roxbury

NUMBER OF VOLUNTEERS: 989

MOST RECENT PUBLICATION: *2% of 2% of All the World's Stories*— a collection of bedtime stories written by 826 Boston after-school students

PROGRAMMING: workshops, in-schools sessions, field trips, publishing projects, after-school tutoring, summer science writing camp, author visits

TUTORING SPACE: 1,335 square feet

STAFF: Leora Silverman Fridman, Daniel Johnson, and Hannah Nolan-Spohn

ITEM NUMBER: 826BOS 100
ITEM NAME: Water Bottle
SPECIFICATIONS: 8" x 3.5" x 3.5"
DESIGNER: Amanda McCorkle
CONCEPT: Wanna Camcam
PRICE: $10.00

NOTES: *Every researcher knows that the first step toward expedition preparedness is an ample water supply. That's why our seemingly banal water bottle is, in fact, the most essential equipment for any Bigfoot seeker. For extended expeditions, be sure to carry two—you never know when you'll need to share.*

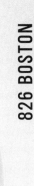

ITEM NUMBER: 826BOS 101
ITEM NAME: Dinner Plate
SPECIFICATIONS: 10"
DESIGNER: Amanda McCorkle
CONCEPT: Megan Dickerson
PRICE: $12.00

NOTES: *When we designed our expedition mess kit, we paid attention to the details that make field dining palatable. Pure melamine GBBRI Institutional Dinnerware is durable, lightweight, and certainly not microwave safe. As the last traces of tikka masala disappear from the plate's smooth surface, Bigfoot's stoic shadow appears, reminding the satiated diner of the bigger picture. An equally suitable choice for wedding china patterns or camp tables, this dinnerware offers proof of the diner's commitment to discovery—and style. Available in puce, hush 'n' wonder purple, monarch orange, and teal.*

149

Career Starter Kit

INSTITUTE'S OWN: ESSENTIALS

Cryptozoology has never been easier!

Best in the Field

ITEM NUMBER: 826BOS 102
ITEM NAME: Career Starter Kit
SPECIFICATIONS: 10" x 5"
DESIGNER: Amanda McCorkle
CONCEPT: Max Greenberg, Ali Reid, Peter Sherer
PRICE: $15.00

NOTES: *The Career Starter Kit was conceived by Institute members driven by a lifelong dream of becoming professional Bigfoot hunters. Designed to provide safe, semi-scientific tools to novice cryptozoologists of all ages, the kit includes tweezers, specimen collecting containers (jar and bag), gloves, magnifying glass, field notebook, and GBBRI pencil.*

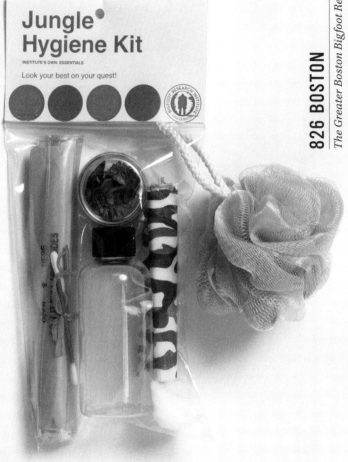

ITEM NUMBER: 826BOS 103
ITEM NAME: Jungle Hygiene Kit
SPECIFICATIONS: 11" x 5"
DESIGNER: Amanda McCorkle
CONCEPT: Max Greenberg, Daniel Johnson, Peter Sherer
PRICE: $20.00

NOTES: *The Jungle Hygiene Kit is modeled on complimentary hotel soaps and offers that users might "look their best on their quest" by maintaining their grooming habits all expedition-long. The set emphasizes careful consideration before use, however. The kit includes a single Q-tip, one yard of camouflage toilet paper, and a very limited amount of soap. Scientists are urged to use it only in pressing circumstances: when heading, for example, to the most important press conference of their lives.*

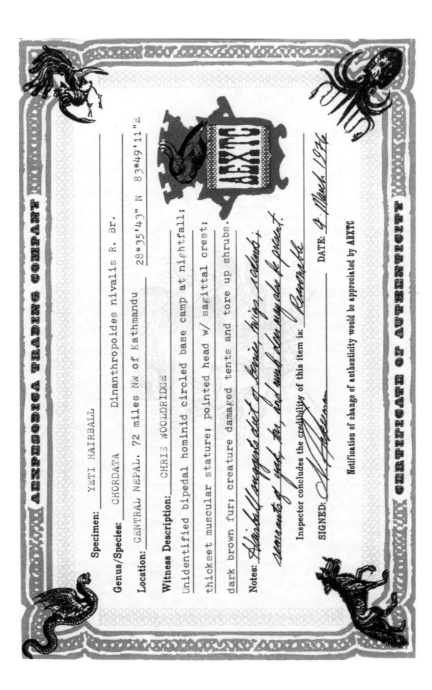

AEXPESODICA TRADING COMPANY
CERTIFICATE OF AUTHENTICITY

Specimen: YETI HAIRBALL

Genus/Species: CHORDATA   Dinanthropoides nivalis R. Br.

Location: CENTRAL NEPAL. 72 miles NW of Kathmandu   28°35'43" N   83°49'11" E

Witness Description: CHRIS WOOLDRIDGE

Unidentified bipedal hominid circled base camp at nightfall; thickset muscular stature; pointed head w/ sagittal crest; dark brown fur; creature damaged tents and tore up shrubs.

Notes: Hairball suggests diet of berries, twigs, rodents; remnants of yeti's dry food must clearly also be present.

Inspector concludes the credibility of this item is: _Reasonable_

SIGNED: _____   **DATE:** 4 March 1994

Notification of change of authenticity would be appreciated by AEXTC

AEXPESODICA TRADING COMPANY

Specimen: YETI HAIRBALL

Genua/Species: CHORDATA   Dinanthropoides nivalis R. Br.

Location: CENTRAL NEPAL. 72 miles NW of Kathmandu   28°35'43" N 83°49'11"£

Witness Description: CHRIS WOOLDRIDGE

Unidentified bipedal hominid circled base camp at nightfall;
thickset muscular stature; pointed head w/ sagittal crest;
dark brown fur; creature damaged tents and tore up shrubs.

Notes: *Hairball suggests diet of berries, twigs, remnants of yak, fur, and much do...*

Inspector concludes the credibility of this item

SIGNED:

Notification of change of authenticity

CERTIFICATE OF

Yeti Hairball
Specimen No. 12   Cont. 1.2 Oz.
Distributed by Aexpesodica Trading Co.
We search so you can research!

ITEM NUMBER: 826BOS 104
ITEM NAME: Yeti Hairball
SPECIFICATIONS: 3.5" x 2" x 1.5"
DESIGNER: Amanda McCorkle
CONCEPT: Daniel Johnson, Peter Sherer
PRICE: $6.00

NOTES: *After extensive research, we have discovered that most cryptids are simply too large to fit into jars. Pieces of cryptids, especially those of the mammalian variety, are unappealing to the public (and to some of the staff as well). The challenge then is to create products that are sufficiently organic, while staying just this side of disgusting. We have, therefore, concentrated on two main areas for our Aexpesodica line: 1) cryptid offspring and 2) cryptid leavings. A certificate of authenticity— complete with a witness sighting and notes from our in-the-field agents—accompanies each specimen.*

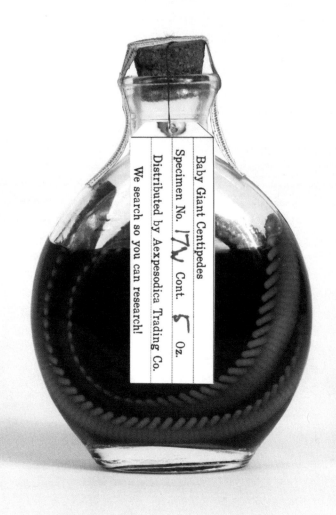

Baby Giant Centipedes

Specimen No. 17W Cont. 5 Oz.

Distributed by Aexpesodica Trading Co.

We search so you can research!

NOTES: *Giant centipedes are invertebrate cryptids that have been observed living in the most remote areas of the Ozark Mountains. How large might these baby giant centipedes have become had they not been captured and preserved by our freelance collectors? That is a question for our customers to ponder as they gaze into the murky liquid of their recent purchase. Unlike many of the other products at the Institute, Baby Giant Centipedes do not make a great gift. Accompanied by a Certificate of Authenticity.*

ITEM NUMBER: 826BOS 105
ITEM NAME: Baby Giant Centipedes
SPECIFICATIONS: 5" x 3.25" x 1"
DESIGNER: Amanda McCorkle
CONCEPT: David Bickham,
Max Greenberg, Peter Sherer
PRICE: $5.00

Sea Serpent Secretions

Specimen No. **17** Cont. **3.2** Oz.

Distributed by Aexpesodica Trading Co.

We search so you can research!

NOTES: *Sea Serpent Secretions are the perfect choice for an entry level purchaser of Aexpesodica. Unlike our Lizardman Hatchings or Mokele-Mbembe Teeth, little or no additional research is required by the purchaser to fully appreciate the uniqueness and absurdity of this item. The goo forms a perfectly flat surface when at rest. Upon inversion of the product, the contents distend slowly downward until equilibrium is reached and the deceptive non-liquid drops as a whole with an audible squish. Accompanied by a Certificate of Authenticity.*

ITEM NUMBER: 826BOS 106
ITEM NAME: Sea Serpent Secretions
SPECIFICATIONS: 4.25" x 3.5" x 1"
DESIGNER: Amanda McCorkle
CONCEPT: David Bickham, Peter Sherer
PRICE: $5.00

ITEM NUMBER: 826BOS 107
ITEM NAME: Kranz & Anderson Canteen
SPECIFICATIONS: 8.5" x 5" x 1.5"
DESIGNER: Amanda McCorkle
CONCEPT: Max Greenberg
PRICE: $5.00

NOTES: *Our Kranz & Anderson line of products probes the strange things that people will do to fill gaping holes in their lives. By relating historical vignettes of danger and intrigue we try to answer the question: what are cryptozoologists really searching for? These product tags feature mock customer recommendations and epic near-death monologues that aim to woo the unsuspecting customer.*

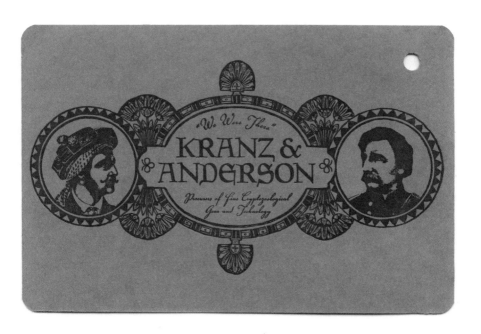

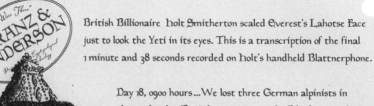

British Billionaire holt Smitherton scaled Everest's Lahotse Face just to look the Yeti in its eyes. This is a transcription of the final 1 minute and 38 seconds recorded on holt's handheld Blattnerphone.

Day 18, 0900 hours…We lost three German alpinists in the avalanche. Buried up to my temples I had to eat the snow away from my head and hands, and then used my Intermediate Cold Weather Cap to scoop free my lower half. I've stripped off my soaked clothes. There is a storm gathering to the north. I worry we may soon have to…
  Do you see that? (faintly audible)…there's something… and hulking 50 meters off…(sound of crampons running)…This is it, at long last!…(low bellow)… Oh my…(end recording).

ITEM NUMBER: 826BOS 108
ITEM NAME: GBBRI Button
SPECIFICATIONS: 2" x 2"
DESIGNER: Amanda McCorkle
CONCEPT: Wanna Camcam
PRICE: $5.00

NOTES: *In my mind, the GBBRI logo needed to feel intriguing, compelling, and soberingly honest. I took my inspiration from* Rambo: First Blood. *I wanted Bigfoot to appear menacing and mysterious, with a tinge of vulnerability. I hoped I had achieved this monumental task, but all was confirmed once I met Loren Coleman, Cryptozoologist Extraordinaire. He congratulated me on presenting Bigfoot in such an earnest and thoughtful way. —Amanda McCorkle*

NOTES: *The T-shirt was the first item that brought the age old adage "Keep it simple, stupid" into sharp focus at the Institute. Researchers were excited to commit to a slogan, something short and sweet, in contrast to our mission statement that states "The Greater Boston Bigfoot Research Institute exists to promote the continuation and expansion of cryptozoological research, both lab-based and in the field..." The T-shirt's front creates a splendid reveal for the person who has been standing in line behind you contemplating the phrase printed on back, "We exist because he exists."*

ITEM NUMBER: 826BOS 001
ITEM NAME: GBBRI T-shirt
SPECIFICATIONS: 100% cotton
DESIGNER: Amanda McCorkle
CONCEPT: Wanna Camcam,
Megan Dickerson,
Daniel Johnson, Peter Sherer
PRICE: $15.00

826 CHICAGO
THE BORING STORE

The ████ ██ ████████ boring █ store ██████ ██ ██ ████ █
is████████ ██ ████ ███ ███ ████ Chicago's ██████
only █████████ ████████ █████████ under
█ cover ██ ███ █ ████ ██████████ secret ████
█ a gent ██████ ████ ██ ████ ████ the
supply ██ ██ ████ ████ █████████ shop ████
███ ███ ████ ████

Interior Architect: Suhail Design · *Interior Design:* Leah Guenther and Patrick Shaffner
Store Front: Chris Ware · *Logo Designer:* Chris Ware
Store Manager: Patrick Shaffner
1331 NORTH MILWAUKEE AVENUE, CHICAGO, ILLINOIS
WWW.826CHI.ORG

826 CHICAGO: PROGRAM OVERVIEW

OPENED: October 2005

SERVES: Chicago Public School District

NEIGHBORHOOD: Wicker Park

NUMBER OF VOLUNTEERS: 1200

MOST RECENT PUBLICATIONS: *Right in Front of Us*—47 stories written by Chicago high school students with a foreword by Alex Kotlowitz

The My World Project—the product of our middle and high school workshop, Photography and Writing, designed and faciliated by National Geographic contract photographer Mike Hettwer

FIELD TRIPS HOSTED: 90 in 2007–08

IN-SCHOOLS SESSIONS: 61 in 2007–08

WORKSHOPS OFFERED: 74 in 2007–08

TOTAL NUMBER OF INDIVIDUAL STUDENTS SERVED: 3545 in 2007–08

TOTAL NUMBER OF STUDENT SESSIONS: 8074 in 2007–08

TUTORING SPACE: 1,580 square feet

STAFF: Pat Mohr, Mara O'Brien, Patrick Shaffner, and Kait Steele

NOTES: *We knew we had to protect our spy-entel's identity upon their leaving our store. Suspicions would rise, for instance, if they were found with a box clearly labeled grappling hook. So, many of our products, like these here, are packed inside mundane brown boxes affixed with a unique label that clearly explains that the contents of the box are indeed not what they may very well be. Let it be noted, too, that our dunnage consists of pre-shredded documents.*

SPECIFICATIONS: 6" x 4" x 3"
TEMPLATE DESIGNER: Chris Ware
CONCEPT: Leah Guenther, Patrick Shaffner, Kait Steele, Chris Ware, Jeremey Wilson

ITEM NUMBER: 826CHI 100
ITEM NAME: Eve's Dropper
PRICE: $6.00

ITEM NUMBER: 826CHI 103
ITEM NAME: Standard Eavesdropper
PRICE: $6.00

ITEM NUMBER: 826CHI 102
ITEM NAME: UV Decoding Pen
PRICE: $9.00

ITEM NUMBER: 826CHI 101
ITEM NAME: Rearview Glasses
PRICE: $8.00

ITEM NUMBER: 826CHI 104
ITEM NAME: Counter Intelligence
SPECIFICATIONS: 9" x 12"
DESIGNERS: Christopher Mitchell,
Patrick Shaffner
PRICE: $5.00

NOTES: *Combining Christopher's graphic design wizardry, my deteriorating knowledge of the Russian language and our mutual love for Chicago's tallest building, a new Chicago intelligence agency and its insignia [seen on this product] were born. The counter samples are acquired through recon(crete) missions to Home Depot. Adhering to my cover story of being a young professional interested in renovating a kitchen, I infiltrate the warehouse, snag some counter samples and exfiltrate them back to headquarters. —Agent Shaffner*

ITEM NUMBER: 826CHI 105
ITEM NAME: Wiretapping Kit
SPECIFICATIONS: 6" x 10" x 3"
TEMPLATE DESIGNER: Chris Ware
CONCEPT: Patrick Shaffner
PRICE: $20.00

NOTES: *The word "tap" is half of my name spelled backwards. This fact, coupled with my exposure, over the years, to wires, granted me the necessary knowledge and authority to produce my own wiretapping kit. This model, covertly used by agents worldwide, is particularly popular with Irish-Americans. Patrick Fitzgerald, the US attorney who caught an Illinois governor attempting to sell a senatorial seat, used the kit to great effect, as did fellow countryman Michael Flatley.*

ITEM NUMBER: 826CHI 106
ITEM NAME: Clandestein
SPECIFICATIONS: 5.5" x 3" x 3" (mug)
TEMPLATE DESIGNER: Chris Ware
CONCEPT: Patrick Shaffner
PRICE: $8.00

NOTES: *No, this section of the catalog is not missing the item's picture. There is actually a product here! You are looking at our Clandestein: the mug that is so secretive, it is invisible. It's a fantastic find for our secret agents because the vessel provides them with the two things they value most: privacy and a potential place for potations.*

On the box label:

The BORING Store

No. 1236. This is not a REDACTOR.

Even if **Redactors** did exist, which they do not, I imagine they would have far too complicated instructions for their usage. Like, 1. Find sensitive information. 2. Press Redactor to beginning of sensitive information. 3. Drag Redactor over sensitive information.

ANOTHER FINE PRODUCT PROCURED FROM

THE BORING STORE

THE LEAST INTRIGUING RETAIL OUTLET IN THE MIDWEST

THE BORING STORE
1331 NORTH MILWAUKEE AVENUE
CHICAGO, ILLINOIS 60622

LIPELESS | BLAND | INSIPID | UNVARIED | DRY

ITEM NUMBER: 826CHI 107
ITEM NAME: Redactor
SPECIFICATIONS: 6" x 4" x 3"
TEMPLATE DESIGNER: Chris Ware
CONCEPT: Patrick Shaffner
PRICE: $3.00

NOTES: *When our secret agents are trying to obscure their most sensitive information, they reach for the Redactor. With ink so dark it's like night itself pours forth from its tip. The Redactor is like an odd highlighter that conceals, rather than illuminating, key pieces of information and only draws attention to, if anything, the user's chary ways and the agent's aversion to openness.*

The BORING Store

No. 13721.
You think this is TRAIL MIX? Get lost!

ATTENTION

Contents
Static
Sensitive

Handling
Precautions
Required.

ULINE
Static Shield Bag

LOT 2058409

NOTES: *To write that this idea struck me while hiking or while on a very dangerous tailing mission would be a lie for I am neither fit nor brave. This is a combination of many items that our spies frequently need from the store. The notebook is weatherproof (take that rain, snow and tears!). The moustaches are cut from a gross of hair fabric, the pencil looks sharp and the GPS often succumbs to the cardinal sin of not finding true north.*

ITEM NUMBER: 826CHI 108
ITEM NAME: Not Trail Mix
SPECIFICATIONS: 7" x 5"
DESIGNER: Patrick Shaffner
PRICE: $12.00

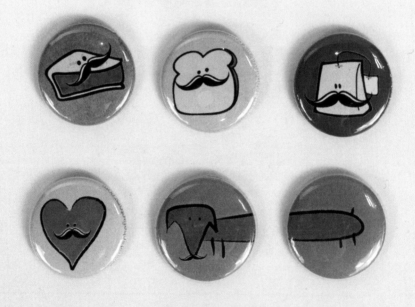

ITEM NUMBER: 826CHI 109
ITEM NAME: Magnetic Force
SPECIFICATIONS: Package 5.75" x 3",
Magnets are 1"
DESIGNER: Nathaniel Davis
PRICE: $10.00 for the set

NOTES: *When a secret agent approached me one day wearing a cleverly disguised (read: moustache festooned) presidential button, I simply had to meet the maker. The maker, it turned out, was standing right next to the buttoned spy. The maker revealed a love of putting moustaches on a motley set of animals, foods, plants, and more. I feel it should be noted that the maker, himself, has not a moustache upon his face. Nor does he have a magnet upon his backside. —Agent Shaffner*

ITEM NUMBER: 826CHI 110
ITEM NAME: Diversion!
Shiny Slip 'Em Ups!
SPECIFICATIONS: 3" x 2.5" x 1"
DESIGNER: Patrick Shaffner
PRICE: $5.00

NOTES: *We needed to package our diversions. Whether they be pictures of cute baby animals, poppable bubble-wrap or shiny, slippery and game-worthy marbles, the container had to be portable and, preferably, pocketable. Jewelry boxes not only met that criteria but, by the use of such a box, we forced a knowing juxtaposition between our product and the normal contents of jewelry boxes thus giving these life saving diversions the air of high quality, importance, extreme wealth, and international human rights issues.*

ITEM NUMBER: 826CHI 111
ITEM NAME: Tote
SPECIFICATIONS: 15" x 15"
DESIGNERS: Dullce and Gabanal
PRICE: $8.00

NOTES: *This masterfully disguised plastic, disposable bag has taken on all the appearances and every quality of an environmentally friendlier cloth tote that you'll think it's just that. And it may be. Emblazoned with Chris Ware's logo, you can stop worrying about wasteful consumer habits and meditate instead on Ware's exquisite artistic craftsmanship. Meditate on this item's beauty. Its balance. Its bagginess.*

ITEM NUMBER: 826CHI 001
ITEM NAME: Boring Store T-shirt
SPECIFICATIONS: 100% cotton
WRITER: Patrick Shaffner
TEMPLATE DESIGNER: Chris Ware
PRICE: $20.00

NOTES: *We'd become so confident of our deceptive packaging, we thought, "Let's make a wearable box, replete with 'This is not a secret agent' label to be worn by our clients themselves." The boxes proved uncomfortable and were absolutely destroyed after one brief cycle in the washing machine. Faring no better being hand-washed, we opted to place the label on a cardboard-colored T-shirt, that, being viewed from a distance gives the appearance of the very boxes of which we're so fond.*

IMAGERY

All product photography, unless otherwise noted, by Eliana Stein.

Boston: Photographs of Greater Boston Bigfoot Research Institute by Mike Ritter. Photographs of writing lab by Daniel Johnson.

Chicago: Photographs of The Boring Store by Gail Reich. Photographs of writing lab by Dan Kuruna.

LA: Photographs of Time Travel Mart by Joel Arquillos (p118–121), Stefan G. Bucher (p122 and p123:bottom), and Jeff Voris (p123: top). Photographs of writing lab by Meiko Takechi Arquillos. Photographs of Shade, Robot Milk, and Professor Clutterbuck's styling products by Stephan G. Bucher.

Michigan: Photograph of Liberty Street Robot Supply & Repair exterior by Gregory Lee. Photographs of LSRSR interior and writing lab by Angi Stevens.

NYC: Photograph of Brooklyn Superhero Supply Co. exterior by Joan Kim. Photographs of BSSC interior by visual-research.com (p46–48 and p49: bottom). Photographs of writing lab by Joe Pacheco (p50: top) and the 826NYC team.

Seattle: Photographs of Space Travel Supply Co. interior by Jon Allred. Photographs of writing lab by Carla Leonardi. Photograph of exterior unknown.

Valencia: Photographs of the Pirate Store by Willy Volk (p12–13) and Justin Carder (p14–15). Photographs of writing lab by Jory John (p16:top) and the 826 Valencia team. Photographs of pirate posters courtesy of Office.

ABOUT 826 NATIONAL

826 National is a family of nonprofit organizations dedicated to helping students, ages 6–18, with expository and creative writing at seven locations across the country. 826 chapters are located in San Francisco, Los Angeles, New York, Chicago, Ann Arbor, Seattle, and Boston.

Our mission is based on the understanding that great leaps in learning can happen with one-on-one attention, and that strong writing skills are fundamental to future success.

Each 826 chapter offers drop-in tutoring, field trips, workshops, and in-schools programs—all free of charge—for students, classes, and schools.

826 is especially committed to supporting teachers, offering services and resources for English language learners, and publishing student work.

To learn more or get involved, please visit
WWW.826NATIONAL.ORG